Clear and Coherent Prose

Clear and Coherent Prose

A Functional Approach

William J. Vande Kopple
Calvin College

Scott, Foresman and Company
Glenview, Illinois   Boston   London

Library of Congress Cataloging-in-Publication Data

Vande Kopple, William.
  Clear and coherent prose : a functional approach / William Vande
Kopple.
      p.   cm.
  Includes index.
  ISBN 0-673-39779-3
  1. English language—Rhetoric.   I. Title.
PE1408.V38 1989
808'.042—dc19   88-15506
                                                                      CIP

1 2 3 4 5 6 7 8 9 10 — KPF — 94 93 92 91 90 89 88

Printed in the United States of America

For Wanda

Preface

The roots of this text are in linguistics. In assumptions and operating procedures, I align myself most closely with linguists of the functional school, represented in Czechoslovakia primarily by Jan Firbas and F. Daneš, in Great Britain and Australia by J. R. Firth and M. A. K. Halliday, and in the United States primarily by Dwight Bolinger, Talmy Givón, and Susumu Kuno. These linguists and their students have developed grammars of the choices available in the English language, choices for structures that have cognitive and emotional effects on readers. To develop such grammars, these linguists have examined language as actually used, trying to relate the functions that people seek to fulfill to the formal means by which they fulfill them. It is such work that has led to other fruitful investigations of language, in subfields of linguistics that have come to have names of their own, such as psycholinguistics and discourse analysis. And it is such work that I draw on to forge connections between linguistics and composition. These connections, I hope, will move us one step closer to an affective stylistics, the study of how language structures affect readers.

In composition studies today, there is much discussion of the rhetorical situation. One of my hopes for this text is that it will make aspects of the rhetorical situation more concrete and vivid for students. I try to demonstrate that choices of sentence forms and essay structures are dependent on many things: on what one's purpose for an essay is, on what situation the essay is a response to, on what knowledge the readers of the essay will probably bring to it. I try to make these aspects clear by means of numerous examples that I have written, excerpts from the work of established writers, discussions of contexts for sentences and short essays, and numerous exercises (many of which include short texts to work on). As students work their way through these examples, excerpts, discussions, and exercises, I believe that they will become better at analyzing and responding to the rhetorical situations they face.

This text can be subdivided into several groups of chapters. Chapter One is a general introduction. Chapters Two through Six all center on the sentence as comprised of a topic and comment. Chapters Seven and Eight take information about topics and comments in individual sentences and extend it to the patterns of topics that writers develop in essays. And Chapters Nine, Ten, and Eleven work on how writers correctly or incorrectly use bits of given and new information in sentences and essays.

Since this text focuses on clarity and coherence, both fundamental concerns in many kinds of writing, it should be useful in several different writing courses. Many of the problems that freshman writers and writers whose first language is not English face, as well as many of those that students in advanced courses in exposition as well as business and technical writing face, are addressed here.

Moreover, this book should lend itself to different manners of use. Individuals can work their way through it, concentrating on the problems that are most acute for them. Teachers can use it in several different ways. They may supplement their main rhetoric with this book and use it to support an occasional lesson on clarity and coherence. Or they may use it to support a unit on clarity and coherence. If the unit must be brief, teachers might not go into all the details of each chapter. Most of the chapters begin with general, more widely applicable matters and move into finer details of style, so that those who are somewhat pressed for time can concentrate on the early parts of chapters. Or teachers may use it as one of the chief texts in a course that focuses on sentence styles and essay structures.

My intellectual debts in this work are numerous, and it is a pleasure to acknowledge the help I have received from the research of the following people: Dwight Bolinger, Roger Cherry, H. H. Clark, Greg Colomb, Allene Cooper, Barbara Couture, Avon Crismore, F. Daneš, George E. Dillon, Nils E. Enkvist, Lester Faigley, Jan Firbas, Peter Fries, Rachel Giora, Talmy Givón, George Goodin, S. E. Haviland, M. A. K. Halliday, David E. Kieras, Daniel Kies, Susumu Kuno, L. Lautamatti, Robert Longacre, Janel Mueller, Kyle Perkins, Ellen Prince, Tanya Reinhart, Leonard F. M. Scinto, Roland Sodowski,

Beth Vander Lei, Teun A. van Dijk, and W. Ross Winterowd. To Joseph M. Williams and Steve Witte I owe a special debt, since their writing has taught me a great deal and since they provided helpful reviews of a draft of this text.

I would also like to thank the students who gave me permission to cite their writing: Tom Bouma, Tammy Brinks, Andrea Clinch, Jamie Grit, Brad Harmon, Laurie Hiemstra, Lisa Hiemstra, Amin Kawar, Steve Kemp, Ross Kool, Jennifer S. Lacy, Kristi Mannes, Carrie Miller, Wendy Pierre, Lori Retsema, Jackie Rosendall, Jennifer Shaw, Siemen Speelman, Marguerite Vande Beek, Jane Vande Polder, Cheryl Vander Weele, Susan Vriesman, Janice Wills, Kurt Wrisley, Joan Zeinstra, and Tim Zoerhoff.

I received excellent help in typing from Michelle De Rose and Alma Walhout. James Vanden Bosch helped me revise and edit; my prose is always the better for Jim's having looked at it. Dean Ward provided invaluable help in proofreading. And throughout the writing process I received great support and encouragement from my family.

Working with people at Scott, Foresman has been instructive and pleasurable. Robert Schwegler was most helpful as I shaped this project from its earliest stages. And Joseph Opiela and Billie Ingram were indispensable to my completing the project. Finally, I would like to thank those at Custom Editorial Productions with whom I worked, Catherine Skintik and Julie Hotchkiss, for their care and attention to detail.

Contents

Clear and Coherent Prose

CHAPTER

1

Understanding the Nature and Aims of This Book

Unlike medicine or the other sciences, writing has no new discoveries to spring on us. We're in no danger of reading in our morning newspaper that a breakthrough has been made in how to write a clear English sentence—that information has been around since the King James Bible.
—William Zinsser, *On Writing Well*, Third Edition

"It's always easier to learn something than to use what you've learned."
—Chaim Potok, *The Promise*

. . . what we hope ever to do with ease we may learn first to do with diligence.
—Samuel Johnson, "Milton," in *Lives of the Poets*

All of us who write struggle frequently to make our prose more coherent. And probably almost as frequently we read prose written by others that is not as coherent as it could be. The following is an example of such prose from a college student:

> Popular music is beneficial to society because it can be used to bring a positive message to people. There are many criticisms of today's music concerning suggestive lyrics. Everything in this world, however, can be twisted and used for evil purposes, but this does not indicate that the thing is bad. For example, nuclear power provides an almost unlimited supply of useful energy in the form of electricity. Because certain persons have used nuclear energy for killing and destruction does not mean that nuclear energy is essentially bad.

Here is another student passage that could be more coherent:

> A part of Chicago was divided up into different parts. Rogers Park, Uptown, Lakeview, Lincoln Park, near Northside, and Hyde Park make up the Goldcoast area. There is a high suicide rate in this area. The Goldcoast area has a high population of people who are sixty-five years and older. They have a high educational level, medium income, medium population per household, and a low amount of unemployment. There is a high percentage of white collar workers and a low proportion of Negroes. Strong external constraints characterize the low suicide areas. The high suicide areas are characterized by weak external constraints. Anomie is common to areas with high suicide rates. This is when people are in a severe state of confusion. Anomic suicide usually results from temporary but abrupt alteration in the norms of society. First, sudden social changes, such as the Great Depression, seemed to be associated with high suicide rates. Second, Durkheim feels that any disturbance in the everyday pattern can lead to an increased suicide rate.

For writing teachers, a big problem with prose such as this is that while it is relatively easy to sense that it is incoherent, it is difficult to understand exactly how it goes wrong. Proper coherence of prose depends on many elements of language working well with each other and with the overall context. Because of the complexity of these relationships, most teachers are limited in their tools for analyzing coherent and incoherent prose, in their terms for describing the coherence or incoherence of prose, and in their advice for remedying incoherent prose.

Therefore, when they describe incoherent prose, teachers often have to rely on vague expressions. I have heard writing teachers say that an essay "doesn't hang together," that a writer is "jumping around," and that a student's method of developing an essay seems to be "scattershot." And when they give advice about how to remedy such situations, they often say little more than "Try to connect this up more" or "Work toward more connections."

Further, most textbooks offer little help in making prose more coherent. Most advise writers to try to repeat key words, to use expressions signaling sequences (*first, next*), to use logical transitions (*therefore*), and to employ parallel structures. It is true that writers of coherent prose often do all of these things. But adding such elements or structures to an essay without regard for other aspects of the structure and meaning of the essay will not necessarily make the essay more coherent. In fact, in some cases doing so can actually make the essay harder to follow, since it can lead readers to look for relationships that are not there.

One of my major goals in this text is to help you see many of the main causes of incoherence. In this process, I hope to equip you with several terms to describe the degree of coherence in an essay and with some ideas about how to make your writing more coherent.

When I use the term *coherence*, I do so to describe prose in which nearly all the sentences have meaningful connections to sentences that appear both before and after them. The terms *cohesion* and *cohesiveness* would probably work just as well to describe such connections. But I use *coherence* to describe these connections and more. I use it to describe essays that function well in the contexts for which their authors write and that will affect readers according to their authors' purposes.

To work toward the goals associated with coherence, I will first try to help you write clearer individual sentences. That is, I hope to help you understand better how you can express information in sentences so that your readers can focus on the information and understand it accurately and efficiently. Once you are able to write such sentences, we will be able to work more easily on writing more coherent essays.

As you become more skilled at writing clear sentences and coherent essays, I hope that you will also develop some other skills and sensitivities. I hope that you will become more sensitive to the stylistic options available in the English language at the same time that you develop a richer vocabulary for talking about these options.

Once you do these things, you will almost certainly become more aware of the fine shades of meaning and subtle emotional effects associated with the various stylistic options. I hope to combat the kind of thinking prevalent among some of my writing students; they think that the way in which they express information makes no difference to readers. I try to convince them—as I will you—that the English language has several slightly different ways of conveying essentially the same information in clauses because each of these ways is appropriate to specific tasks in specific situations.

As you learn more about the relationship between the forms of language and their functions, you should become increasingly able to respond skillfully to the writing tasks that you face. Specifically, you should become more concerned with and precise about what you want your writing to accomplish. You should more readily examine your subject matter from various points of view and learn from this examination. And you should become better at analyzing how much your readers know about your subject matter and how much they need to learn about it from your writing.

Learning such things and displaying such skills are not all that you need to do to become a skilled writer. Writing skillfully demands a multitude of abilities, some of which will perhaps always be rather mysterious to us. But in my experience working with student and professional writers, once people learn to write clear sentences and coherent essays, and if along the way they refine their stylistic and rhetorical sensibilities, they are usually able to produce effective essays in various situations.

As the title of this book indicates, the approach that I take to style and writing is a functional one. Technically, this means that my approach rests on work done by functional linguists, so called because they originally investigated the general functions of language. The general function that we will be most concerned with here is that of communicating information about the world. Another general function is that of establishing and maintaining interpersonal relationships.

From these investigations, functional linguists went on to examine how units of language—usually the clause—fulfill the general functions of language. Here a second meaning of the word *function* comes in, since these linguists divided sentences into parts that have important functions in the processes of communication. They went beyond identifying and labeling parts of or structures within sentences. They asked, "What do the parts do? How do they function in moving the communication along?" In this work, they identified parts of sentences that serve as focal points for readers and other parts that convey information about the focal points.

Finally, a few words about how I will proceed in this book. The unit that I will investigate in most detail is the independent clause. You should not equate the words *independent clause* with *sentence* because groups of words punctuated as sentences often are made up of more than an independent clause. But much of what I write about sentences made up of one independent clause can be extended to sentences made up of an independent clause and one or more dependent clauses. Further, in Chapters Two and Six, I extend comments about sentences made up of one independent clause to longer and more complex sentences.

Generally I assume a rudimentary knowledge of grammar and grammatical terms on your part, although I provide a glossary of grammatical terms at the end of the book to supply information you may have forgotten. Also, when grammatical concepts become more complex, I try to provide more explanation.

Throughout the book, I draw examples of sentences from many different sources. Occasionally I draw from works of fiction, and sometimes from conversations I have participated in. I do so only when the sentence structure being examined functions essentially in the same way no matter where it is found, whether in expository essay, mystery novel, or casual conversation.

Finally, I offer general guidelines, not rigid rules, about prose style. These guidelines are based on tendencies—sometimes strong tendencies—in the English language, which means that usually you should follow the guidelines. Sometimes, however, you will have good reasons to ignore one or more of the guidelines. And all the while you should realize that making stylistic choices frequently costs you. For example, we will see in Chapter Three that using a passive verb can often help you maintain coherence in a passage.

But deciding to use a passive verb will also cost you—you will have to use more words than with an active verb, and you will lose some of the vigorous movement that an active verb would bring. In such a case, however, the coherence of the passage would probably count for more, and you would choose the passive verb.

One of the keys to skilled writing is making such decisions so that you consistently gain more than you lose. I hope that this book will help you do so.

CHAPTER

Identifying Topics and Comments in Sentences

In rhetoric, the flexibility of English sentences contributes in a major way to the elegance and readability of discourse.

> —Frederick Bowers,
> "Meaning and Sentence Structure"

If alternatives exist, then they serve different purposes.
> —Frank Smith, *Writing and the Writer*

One can see certain analogies in this kind of brain specialization between the special ways that tools are used and sentences are constructed. With tools, the left hand develops a holding grip while the right develops various precision grips—it "does something to" what is held in the left hand. A propositional sentence contains a topic (usually the grammatical subject) and a comment (usually the grammatical predicate), which does something to or tells something about the topic. . . . In a discourse, the topic is often "held over"—our imagery suggests the analogy with handedness.

> —Dwight Bolinger and Donald A. Sears,
> *Aspects of Language*, Third Edition

> . . . words at the beginning [of sentences] are long and loud, partly to cue beginningness, but also to convey information about what's to come; and what's not to.
> —Harvey B. Sarles, *Language and Human Nature*

> To write is to affirm at the very least the superiority of this *order* over that *order*.
> —Wayne C. Booth, *The Rhetoric of Fiction*, First Edition

To begin working toward clarity and coherence, please imagine the following scene with me: My colleague Jim, who is using his new graphite racquet, begins our weekly racquetball match by hitting the ball so hard that he cracks the ball in half.

Now suppose that in some context I must describe Jim's action in one written sentence. I would have many different sentence forms to choose from. Each of these would convey essentially the same information as the others. But each would package that information in a slightly different way. In other words, each sentence would present the same action from a slightly different perspective.

For example, I could choose from at least the following forms:

Jim cracked the ball with his new graphite racquet.

The ball was cracked by Jim with his new graphite racquet.

As for the ball, Jim cracked it with his new graphite racquet.

As for his new graphite racquet, Jim used it to crack the ball.

The ball Jim cracked with his new graphite racquet.

His new graphite racquet Jim used to crack the ball.

What Jim did was to crack the ball with his new graphite racquet.

What Jim cracked with his new graphite racquet was the ball.

What Jim used to crack the ball was his new graphite racquet.

The one who cracked the ball with his new graphite racquet is Jim.

The thing that Jim cracked with his new graphite racquet was the ball.

The thing that Jim used to crack the ball was his new graphite racquet.

It was Jim who cracked the ball with his new graphite racquet.

It was the ball that Jim cracked with his new graphite racquet.

It was his new graphite racquet that Jim used to crack the ball.

By now you have probably anticipated my question: How should I decide which one of these forms to use? Some people might answer by noting that some of these forms appear far less often in print than others do, and that therefore they should not be selected. Other people would argue that the shortest form is the best. But neither response helps us choose among forms that are equal in length and frequency.

Of course, in the strictest sense, I have presented an impossible challenge here. To be able to answer the question fully, one would have to know a great deal about the situation in which I would be writing: why I am writing; for whom I am writing; what those people know about Jim, me, and racquetball; and what they most likely need to know about us and our racquetball matches in order for me to achieve my purpose.

But even without full knowledge of purpose and audience, it is possible to begin to say pertinent things about which of the forms I should use in a particular place in an essay.

One could do so by considering the forms in the light of what I will call "aboutness." That is, even though all the forms describe the same activity, many are messages about different things. They hold up different things for readers to learn about. They focus on different things.

For example, even without knowing much about the situation in which *Jim cracked the ball with his new graphite racquet* is used, most people would say that it is a message about Jim. Most would say that *The ball was cracked by Jim with his new graphite racquet* is a message about the ball. And most would say that *What Jim did was to crack the ball with his new graphite racquet* is a message about what Jim did.

SENTENCE TOPICS

I will call the part of a sentence that tells what the sentence is about the *topic*. In each sentence, something is topicalized. In the three sentences that we just looked at, *Jim*, *The ball*, and *What Jim did* are the topics, respectively.

To expand a little on this definition, I would add that the topic of a sentence is its center of attention or its focal point. The topic of a sentence shows what perspective on events or actions its writer is taking.

For instance, *Jim cracked the ball with his new graphite racquet* reveals a writer treating an action by focusing on Jim. On the other hand, *The ball was cracked by Jim with his new graphite racquet* reveals a writer treating the same action but by focusing on the ball.

It is impossible to predict where the topics of all sentences will appear. But in most sentences of well-written prose, the topic appears early. It is usually the first noun or noun phrase. And it is often identical to what traditional grammar calls the subject and its modifiers. The subject of a sentence is generally the element or elements with which the verb agrees in person and number. In *Jim cracked the ball with his new graphite racquet*, *Jim* is the subject; it is also the topic.

The correspondence between subject and topic does not hold in all sentences. For example, consider especially the third of the following sentences:

> For our trip to Glacier National Park, Steve bought new boots and a new rucksack. The boots he wore every day. The rucksack he never took out of the van.

In the third sentence, *The rucksack* is the topic. This sentence is a message about the rucksack. And here *The rucksack* is the direct object of the sentence, not its subject.

The correspondence between subject and topic does not hold in other sentence forms. For example, in a sentence made up of two clauses, the first of which gives the source of the information conveyed in the second (*He said that the comet struck the satellite*), the subject of the main clause is *He*. But we would miss an important characteristic of messages if we were to say that this sentence is about the person to whom *He* refers. This sentence is basically a message about *the comet*; thus here, too, the subject and the topic are not identical.

We are now nearly ready to begin answering the question that I posed earlier. We could begin deciding which sentence form to use in an essay by learning what perspective on the action in the racquetball court that it requires, by deciding what the essay is about. Then we could choose the form or forms that focus on the racquetball incident in the way appropriate to the essay.

For example, if Jim has been the consistent focus in the essay, I should select a form that has *Jim* as its topic. I should avoid a form that has as its topic *the ball* or *his graphite racquet*. That would throw the essay out of focus.

SENTENCE COMMENTS

But there is more to the answer. The topic indicates what the sentence is a message about. But the sentence also conveys information about the topic. The elements in a sentence that say something about the topic I will call the *comment*. Generally, these elements correspond to the complete predicate. If a sentence were read aloud, the main emphasis would usually fall within the comment.

For instance, in *The ball was cracked by Jim with his new graphite racquet*, the topic is *The ball*, and the comment includes everything after it. In *Jim cracked the ball with his new graphite racquet*, on the other hand, *Jim* is the topic, and *cracked the ball with his new graphite racquet* is the comment.

TESTS TO DISTINGUISH TOPICS FROM COMMENTS

I have indicated that the topic of a sentence usually appears early in it and corresponds to the subject. I have also noted that the comment usually appears later, corresponds to the full predicate, and includes the main emphasis of a sentence. These are helpful general descriptions, but they are not the most precise. There are other methods, though, that can help distinguish topics from comments in many sentences.

The Question-Test

One of these is the question-test. It involves imagining what question the sentence we are concerned with could be thought of as providing an answer to.

For example, consider the following sentences:

John is one of my really close friends.
He teaches in a suburban high school.

Imagine that we have to determine what the topic and comment of the second sentence are. We could start by imagining what question this sentence would be a logical response to. The key to this is coming up with a verb that is more general than the one in the sentence (*teaches*).

The question that I would formulate is, "What does John do?" To this, *He teaches in a suburban high school* seems to be a very logical response. Next we have to determine what is referred to in both the imagined question and the response. That is the topic of the response. In this case John is referred to in both. Thus *He*, which replaces John in the response, is the topic of that sentence.

Now we must return to the question. We pick out from it the interrogative element (*What*) and the verb (*does do*). If we put these together to make another (admittedly rough-sounding) question, we get *What does do*? The words from the response that answer this question or provide a more specific correspondence to it (*teaches in a suburban high school*) make up the comment of that sentence.

The question-test also works well for sentences such as *The rucksack he never took out of the van*. Recall that this sentence appeared earlier in the following context:

> For our trip to Glacier National Park, Steve bought new boots and a new rucksack. The boots he wore every day. The rucksack he never took out of the van.

Imagine reading only the first two of these sentences and then stopping. What question would be on your mind? Probably something like "OK, I know about the boots. But what happened to the rucksack?" *The rucksack he never took out of the van* is an appropriate answer to that question.

The element that is common to both the question and the answer is *rucksack*. It, therefore, is the topic of the sentence being considered. The answer to "What happened?" is *he never took (it) out of the van*. These elements make up the comment.

The Challenge-Test

The second method of distinguishing topics from comments is the lie-test or challenge-test. It involves determining what part of a sentence readers would probably not call a lie or challenge. That part is the topic. Readers pay excellent attention to it, but they do so to become oriented to what the sentence is about. They do not usually ask whether it is true. This test also involves determining what part of a sentence readers would consider calling a lie or challenging. That part is the comment.

For instance, look again at two sentences that we examined earlier:

> John is one of my really close friends.
>
> He teaches in a suburban high school.

Imagine that we have to decide what the topic and comment of the second sentence are without using the question-test.

We can start by asking whether readers would likely consider challenging the *He*. No. They would not be inclined to read the second sentence and respond by saying, "No, it's not John, it's Vern," or "That's a lie; Vern does." Therefore, we can classify *He* as the topic of this sentence.

On the other hand, once readers finish this sentence, they might be inclined to challenge all that appears after *He*. It is possible to imagine readers saying, "That's not what he does. He administers the local community college." All that appears after *He*, then, is the comment.

Try the challenge-test with another sentence that we looked at earlier: *The rucksack he never took out of the van.* When readers encounter this sentence, they would not be likely to say, "No, that's not true; it was the water bottle that he never took out of the van."

However, they might be inclined to say, "No, that's not true; he took it out at least once, that time we stopped in West Glacier." If they did respond in this way, they would be challenging information conveyed in the comment.

Exercise One

Decide what the topic and comment of each of the following sentences are. Especially since these sentences can make up a short paragraph, you probably can make sound decisions about topics and comments. Practice several methods of determining topics and comments: Look for the correspondence between topics and subjects, comments and predicates; use the question-test; and use the challenge test.

1. Commencement Day began with a breakfast for the graduates, their guests, and some faculty members.
2. The graduates and their guests seemed to be in a very festive mood.
3. As for the faculty members, they seemed to feel a little out of place.
4. Most of the formal ceremonies were handled by the president of the senior class.
5. It was he who gave a very moving tribute to the college.
6. That tribute he gave with some slight quavering in his voice.
7. What he tried to make clear was how much his teachers had helped him move toward true discernment.
8. After the tribute, the podium was turned over to an officer of the alumni association.
9. What he said both shocked and irritated the graduates.
10. In essence, his request was for them to start sending financial contributions to the college.

Exercise Two

A few summers ago my son Jonathan, while fishing, caught a large rock bass on a bare hook. Try to describe that action in one sentence. But in different sentences, you should topicalize different things.

For example, if you were asked to topicalize Jonathan, you should write *Jonathan caught a large rock bass with a bare hook.*

1. Topicalize *a large rock bass.*
2. Topicalize *a bare hook.*

Now describe the same activity, but do so by completing sentences that begin as follows:

3. As for that large rock bass,
4. The one who caught
5. As for Jonathan,
6. What Jonathan did
7. That rock bass
8. It was a rock bass that
9. It was Jonathan who

TOPICS AND COMMENTS IN SENTENCES WITH MORE THAN ONE CLAUSE

When we move from sentences composed of one independent clause to those made up of several clauses, some of which may be dependent clauses, the situation with topics and comments becomes more complicated.

It is only slightly more complicated with compound sentences. Each independent clause has its own topic and comment. For example, consider *I went to the store, but I did not find the spices.* In the first clause, *I* is the topic and *went to the store* is the comment. In the second clause, *I* is the topic and *did not find the spices* is the comment.

With sentences that contain a dependent clause, we could get very technical since in the strictest sense each dependent clause has its own topic and comment. But such an analysis is probably more complicated than we need.

Therefore, I will treat dependent clauses in the following manner. If a noun clause serves as the subject of a sentence, it will probably be the topic for that sentence, e.g., *That we asked for an extension* (topic) *surprised them* (comment). If the noun clause appears after the verb— as a direct object, indirect object, objective complement, object of a preposition, or in apposition to a noun—it will probably be part of the comment: *We* (topic) *should give the books to whoever wants them* (comment).

Adjective clauses usually modify nouns or pronouns. If the word that an adjective clause modifies is part of the topic of a sentence, the adjective clause will also be part of the topic, e.g., *The boy who sailed beyond the end of the pier* (topic) *looked weak* (comment). On the other hand, if the word that the adjective clause modifies is part of the comment, the adjective clause will also be part of the comment, e.g., *She* (topic) *wrote the only book that is used in all law schools* (comment).

Finally, if an adverbial clause precedes an independent clause, we sense that on one level it serves as the topic while the whole main clause serves as a comment. But because this analysis is more delicate than we need for writing instruction, I will treat the adverbial as introducing the main clause: *Since the dune was long and steep* (introductory adverbial), *he* (topic) *decided to wait at the bottom* (comment). If an adverbial clause follows the main-clause subject of a sentence, I will treat it as part of the comment: *The large sailboat* (topic), *although it was not leaking very badly, had to be towed to port* (comment). And I will treat an adverbial clause that concludes a sentence as part of the comment, e.g., He (topic) *swam to shore, although he had cramps in both of his calves* (comment).

SENTENCE TOPICS AND ETHICS, PART I

Readers apparently accept the topic of a sentence as something beyond challenging, and—if they are inclined to challenge something—challenge the comment. Once writers realize this, they must beware of writing in ways that verge on or fall into the realm of the unethical. By including information in their sentence topics that could or should be challenged, they can trick their readers into accepting it. They might very well not be able to get readers to accept the same information if they were to express it in a sentence comment.

For example, a shrewd and somewhat unscrupulous car dealer probably would not say the following about a car: "I also have this car for sale. It is peppy and yet very fuel efficient." If the dealer were to do so, he or she would be expressing the claim that the car is peppy and yet very fuel efficient in a sentence comment, where it might invite challenges.

Instead, the dealer would probably say something like, "This peppy and very fuel-efficient car is also for sale." Do you see—or maybe even feel—the difference? In this sentence, the dealer treats the information about the pep and fuel efficiency of the car as undeniable. And prospective buyers might be tricked into accepting that information. What does the dealer treat as deniable? That he or she has this car for sale, something that is so obvious that no one would consider challenging it.

Similarly, can you imagine a politician claiming that "My extremist and short-sighted opponent has appeared on television twice in the last week"? I can. What is she or he doing? Smuggling the claims centering on *extremist* and *short-sighted* into the sentence topic, where hearers will be likely to accept them, and including in the comment information that no one would be likely to challenge.

Once you know about such potential seductions, you should be better prepared to cope with some advertisements. Some of them go beyond anything we have examined so far because they do not even include comments. We see or hear topics, sometimes fairly complex topics. We encounter clusters of words such as *fresh, sparkling, refreshing wine coolers*, not *These wine coolers are fresh, sparkling, and refreshing*. Or we read about *a special limited-time offer* (not *This offer is special and runs for a limited time*), or about a *thirty-day, no-risk, free trial* (not *This trial is for thirty days, carries no risk, and is free*).

Also operating here, of course, is our tendency not to question adjectives that appear before nouns, but to question those adjectives if they appear after verbs, where they call attention to themselves because they seem to be close to the point of the sentence. We tend to accept modifiers if they are simply attached to something that we know exists (*This exquisite purity*). We might question the same modifier if it were predicated about that which we know exists (*This purity is exquisite*).

Exercise Three

Below are some statements that could conceivably appear in political or advertising campaigns. Some of these include in their topics information that might not belong there. Others of them do little or no such smuggling. Decide which ones you think smuggle information into topics, tell what information is being smuggled, and estimate how serious you think each case of smuggling is.

For example, the sentence *My degenerate opponent will not represent you well* smuggles *degenerate* into its topic. Without further evidence, or if this is untrue, this would be a serious misuse of language.

1. Sensational clothing bargains are available at Primarily Pants each day until midnight.
2. This lawnmower starts with just one pull, runs smoothly, and gives your lawn a smooth, clean cut.
3. Our best model is on sale through Memorial Day for a drastically reduced price.
4. Jules Alexander: for a better tomorrow.
5. Today's deluxe filters—all the pleasure of cigarette taste with absolutely no tar.
6. The governor pays far too little attention to the well-being of this side of the state.
7. My opponent and his backward-looking supporters are proposing that we decrease taxes.

8. Invisible braces for a new you.
9. World-class skis at the lowest prices anywhere.
10. What our state desperately needs is more jobs.

TO REVIEW:
A FUNCTIONAL VIEW OF SENTENCES

What we have begun to develop is a functional view of sentences. As messages, sentences consist of two parts.

One of these, the topic, the writer holds up before readers as if to say, "Consider this. It's what I'm going to communicate to you about." The necessity of having topics for sentences is obvious. We always have trouble when we are not sure what someone is writing or talking about. Thus we often hear people in conversations saying things like, "Pardon me. Who's this about? What's this about?"

Moreover, since topics usually appear early in sentences, they keep readers from wondering or being uneasy for very long. And since skilled writers normally use topics to hold up before their readers things that the readers often know something about or can recognize, topics help make communication efficient. They connect what readers need or want to learn to what they already know.

The other part of the sentence, the comment, adds the information about the topic. In using comments, writers say, "Here's what I want you to know about the topic I've called to your attention."

When we view sentences in this way, we realize that they reveal what perspectives writers are taking on things; we realize how writers have decided to package information about the world. Writers can write about one event or action in several different ways. They can select different focal points (topics) and different things to convey about these focal points (comments).

As we will see later, if writers make these selections wisely, it is probably because they keep in mind what they are trying to accomplish with their essays, what sets of focal points they have established up to certain points in their essays, what their readers already know about given subjects, and what these readers still need to learn about the subjects. As you make informed decisions about sentence topics and comments, you should develop more control over your style, more power in your prose, and more joy in using the resources of written language appropriately.

FURTHER READING

Readers who wish to investigate some of the experimental and theoretical research underlying this chapter may wish to consult the following works. I have kept the number of entries to a minimum; these are the works I would recommend that others start with.

Bolinger, D. (1980). *Language—The Loaded Weapon*. London and New York: Longman.

Firbas, J. (1982). "Has Every Sentence a Theme and a Rheme?" In J. Anderson (Ed.), *Language Form and Linguistic Variation* (pp. 97-115). Amsterdam: John Benjamins.

Firbas, J. (1986). "On the Dynamics of Written Communication in the Light of the Theory of Functional Sentence Perspective." In C. R. Cooper & S. Greenbaum (Eds.), *Studying Writing: Linguistic Approaches* (pp. 40-71). Beverly Hills: Sage Publications.

Halliday, M. A. K. (1967). "Notes on Transitivity and Theme in English, Part Two," *Journal of Linguistics, 3*, 199-244.

Kuno, S. (1972). "Functional Sentence Perspective: A Case Study from Japanese and English," *Linguistic Inquiry, 3*, 269-320.

Van Dijk, Teun A. (1977). "Topic, Comment, Focus, and Their Functions in Discourse," *Text and Context: Explorations in the Semantics and Pragmatics of Discourse*. London: Longman.

CHAPTER

Selecting Appropriate Sentence Topics

. . . and it is a narrow mind which cannot look at a subject from various points of view.
—George Eliot, *Middlemarch*

Language necessarily imposes a perspective in which things are viewed. . . .
—Jerome Bruner, "The Language of Education"

There is, when we reflect upon the matter, a certain morality in clarity of thought. . . .
—Richard M. Weaver, *The Ethics of Rhetoric*

Words are for those with promises to keep.
—W. H. Auden, "Their Lonely Betters"

Indeed at the Nuremberg trials each of the SS defendants justified his behavior during the war with great tenacity. They had acted, so they claimed, in a spirit of self-sacrifice and had done their jobs conscientiously. They were only too ready to agree that "the war entailed much suffering," but by phrasing it in this passive way, they implied that they could not be regarded as active instruments in that process.
—G. S. Graber, *History of the SS*

Now that we have explored how to identify topics and comments in sentences, we are ready to move to a general guideline for clear and coherent writing, and to use that guideline to pursue further the question that I used to introduce Chapter Two.

THE FIRST GUIDELINE

The first guideline is as follows: In context, select appropriate topics for your sentences.

The first guideline directs us to consider what a particular sentence should be about and then to express that in the sentence topic. But how do we know what a sentence should be about?

The answer lies in having a consistent focal point throughout an essay. In well-written prose, readers normally expect the topic of a sentence to be identical to, similar to, reasonably closely related to, or a part of the same scenario or field of meaning as that of topics they have already read in the essay as a whole or in the section of the essay in which the sentence appears. As we will see in greater detail in Chapter Seven, readers expect sections of essays or whole essays to be about the same thing or closely related things; they expect one topic to be similar to the preceding topics or comments. If one topic is not similar to preceding topics, readers expect it to be similar to material in an earlier comment.

The psychological principle that I am touching on here is one that affects experiences for all of us: It is easier to attend to and understand something (not just written language) if the points we are asked to focus our attention on change neither frequently nor without good reason.

We can find some evidence that readers expect topics to be identical or logically related across sentences in the following pair of sentences:

Henry saw Clare yesterday.

He told him about the contest.

In these sentences no clues help us associate *He* with *Henry* and *him* with *Clare*. But we make these associations readily. What operates here is that, unless we have a good reason not to, we assume that the topic of the second sentence will be identical or similar to the topic of the first. And it is.

To explore some of the implications of the first guideline, we should take another look at some of the sample sentences from the beginning of Chapter Two. The following three will serve well:

Jim cracked the ball with his new graphite racquet.

The ball was cracked by Jim with his new graphite racquet.

What Jim did was to crack the ball with his new graphite racquet.

Now consider the following short paragraph:

Jim is probably the most powerful racquetball player in our department. He serves so hard that he frequently scores service aces. He hits ceiling shots that go over all but the tallest player's head. He hits passing shots that are difficult to get a racquet on. And just last week . . .

Which of the three sentences would you use to conclude this paragraph? I would select the first. Why? Because all of the sentences before the last one focus on Jim. This paragraph is about Jim—more specifically about his power in racquetball. *Jim* or *He* appears in all of the topics before the last sentence. Thus readers would expect the last sentence to have a topic identical or closely related to *Jim*.

To insert the second sample sentence into this slot, on the other hand, would produce a somewhat jarring and disorienting experience for readers. Try reading this paragraph with the second sample sentence at the end. You should feel a little jolt as the topics move from *Jim*, *He*, *He*, and *He* to *the ball*.

But this does not make *The ball was cracked by Jim with his new graphite racquet* a sentence that should never be used. On the contrary, it would be the preferred one in a paragraph in which all the sentences package information in such a way that focusing on *the ball* is natural.

For example, this sentence would be preferred at the end of the following paragraph:

> I bought several pieces of new racquetball equipment last month.
> Now they are all ruined. The racquet shattered when I tried to scrape a
> shot off the wall. The court shoes no longer have good tread left on
> them. And . . .

Here you could consider inserting *Jim cracked the ball with his new
graphite racquet*. It is grammatically correct. But it would not function
well. It would throw the paragraph out of its focus on the pieces of
racquetball equipment. If it were used, the last few topics would
move from *The racquet* to *The court shoes* to *Jim*. Using a sentence
that topicalizes *The ball* rather than *Jim* makes the set of topics in the
paragraph more logically related and coherent.

How about the third of the sample sentences (*What Jim did was to
crack the ball with his new graphite racquet*)? Earlier you might have
suggested it as a good filler for the final slot in the first paragraph we
looked at. And in some respects it would have worked there. But
sentences of this form usually have special functions, one of which is
to mark contrasts between one thing or action and several others.

To make this clearer, consider another short paragraph:

> When Jim tested the new racquetballs and his new graphite racquet
> last week, he could have tried several things. He could have hit some
> easy ceiling shots. He could have tried some soft cross-court serves. Or
> he could even have volleyed the ball gently from backcourt. But . . .

In this context the sentence beginning with *What Jim did* is perfectly
natural, more appropriate than either of the other two sentences.

In sum, as you think of material to write and as you edit your
writing, examine the context of the sentence that you are working on
and try to keep its topic identical to or logically related to those that
you have already written. Another good option is to try to keep its
topic related to an earlier comment, as is true of these two sentences:

> We could not find her watch.
> It had been lying on the beach towel.

Of course, as we shall see in Chapter Seven, you will not be able to
do this all of the time. There are points in all essays when writers
have to introduce topics that may be only loosely related to
preceding topics and comments. This happens most often at the
beginning of paragraphs or larger subsections of essays. But when
you introduce such topics, you should realize that you are doing so
and have a good reason for it. Perhaps you will have to draw your

readers' attention to the fact that you are doing so. Otherwise, they may experience annoying jolts as they jump from one topic to an unexpected one to yet another unrelated one.

Such unjustified shifting of topics is, I believe, the root cause of other problems in writing that are usually discussed without any reference to sentence topics. For example, think about what many textbooks label a shift in voice, when the verbs in consecutive clauses shift from active to passive voice, or *vice versa*. Such a shift occurs in the following:

> *We tiptoed to the edge of the pond.* (active voice)
>
> *Bass could be heard jumping in the shallows.* (passive voice)

Many textbooks attack such shifts by pointing out the different voices and instructing students to be consistent in the voice of verbs used so close to each other. I think, though, that the fundamental problem here is one of an unjustified shift in topics. The writer switches topics, from *We* to *Bass*. And that switch entails a switch in the voice of the accompanying verbs. If the writer had kept a consistent focal point in these two sentences, for example on the *We*, the shift in voice would not occur. (*We heard bass jumping in the shallows.*)

Exercise One

After you read each of the following paragraphs, decide which of the two subsequent sentences works better as the last sentence of the paragraph. Be prepared to defend your decisions.

For example, consider the following short paragraph and two subsequent sentences:

> Tinker's Restaurant is a favorite with visitors to Michigan's Upper Peninsula. The chef is renowned for his specialty, Lake Superior whitefish. And all the waiters are pleased to fill visitors in on the folklore of the surrounding region.
>
> a. Tinker's is located only seven miles north of highway M-28.
> b. Highway M-28 is only seven miles south of Tinker's.

Here you should select the first sentence to conclude the paragraph. Its topic (*Tinker's*) is identical to or closely related to all the others in the paragraph. The topic of the second sentence (*Highway M-28*), on the other hand, is not directly related to any of the earlier topics or comments in the paragraph.

1. This book of short poems has gone through several revisions recently. New introductions for the five sections have been written. Several modern poems have been added, and some of the less popular old ones have been deleted. All of the translated poems have been reexamined to ensure their faithfulness to the originals.
   a. And James B. Smarm & Sons, Inc., has set the collection in a new typeface.
   b. And the collection has been set in a new typeface by James B. Smarm & Sons, Inc.

2. The trail to the top of Mt. Katahdin looks easy but is actually extremely challenging. It begins gently enough, winding its way through stands of northern conifers. But soon it becomes very difficult. It approaches a steep rockslide and then goes straight up it. Above the rockslide it is not quite as steep.
   a. But it becomes more dangerous because it skirts crevasses with sheer walls.
   b. But crevasses with sheer walls right next to it make it more dangerous

3. The National Park Service has hired a new airplane company to fly people to and from Isle Royale. The old company had only two planes, and frequently one of them would be in the hangar for repairs. The new company operates six planes. These are all modern models and should require very little maintenance.
   a. In addition, the new company has hired commercial pilots with a wealth of flying experience.
   b. In addition, commercial pilots with a wealth of flying experience have been hired by the new company.

4. For our fishing trip to Sugar Island, I bought some new fishing line, some new lures, and lots of mosquito repellant. The line I needed desperately since my old line was becoming snarled all the time. Most of the lures I needed, too, since I had recently lost some of my old favorites.
   a. However, the spring in the north had been very cold, and therefore I did not need the mosquito repellant.
   b. However, the mosquito repellant I did not need, since the spring in the north had been very cold.

5. The women's volleyball team has done very well in the past three years. The players have excellent abilities and can hit all the necessary shots.

They can bump from the backcourt, set from the midcourt, and spike from the front line. In addition, the players have excellent attitudes toward themselves and their opponents. They are not jealous of each other and work hard to develop each other's skills. They are cordial and encouraging to their opponents.

a. Indeed, the college has been represented very well by them.

b. Indeed, they have represented the college very well.

Exercise Two

Add a sentence or two of your own—sentences with appropriate topics—to the end of each of the following clusters of sentences. For example, consider the following short cluster:

> Walden Pond is by no means the tranquil place that Thoreau knew. It now has a swimming area, and near it one hears toddlers' squeals and parents' warnings about staying near shore.

To this cluster you could add a sentence such as *In addition, its shoreline now serves as a racecourse for off-road vehicles*, since it topicalizes *its shoreline*, which is closely related to the earlier topics.

1. The Cycling Club is sponsoring some very appealing bike trips this summer. One is called the "Dunes Scooter." It begins in Northport and goes down the coast of Lake Michigan to Grand Haven. Another is called the "Ontonagon Frolic." It starts in the Porcupine Mountains and finishes in Mackinaw City.

2. Jonson and Knick made an excellent research team. Jonson had an excellent theoretical mind and was very patient.

3. Many college students have a difficult time finding a summer job. Some of them do not get out of school until June, when many of the jobs are already gone. Some of them live in states with depressed economies.

4. For bait, he bought some leeches and some crayfish. The leeches were meant for bass.

5. A successful dramatic tragedy is dependent on several things. In the first place, it requires viewers who can have heroes. Second, it demands that its viewers take some things in life very seriously. They should have firm beliefs about reality.

6. One of the more significant aspects of writing is the process of invention. *Invention* basically refers to the ways in which people think

of material to write. That material often wells up out of their subconscious mind.

7. Montana is a state of striking landscapes. Some of the sandy hill country in the east resembles the surface of the moon. The east side of the Rocky Mountains is dry, with only sparse vegetation.

8. He had come to college thinking that he wanted to prepare for graduate business school. But early in his college career he took a course in linguistics.

9. Hamlet's problem has nothing to do with his inability to make a decision. It has to do with his relationship with his parents.

10. Not all critics give *The Cosby Show* unqualified praise. Some say that the younger actors' performances are stilted.

TOPICS: PERSONAL OR CONCEPTUAL?

So far I have stressed that as you think of material to write and as you edit that material, you should try to establish a consistent focal point throughout essays or larger portions of them.

But I have written little about what exactly those topics should be, about what they should refer to. And I cannot write very much, since what you topicalize in the sentences of a particular essay will depend on your overall subject, on who your readers are, and on why you are writing.

I can, however, begin to offer some advice about what in many cases you should and should not topicalize. Some of this advice is based on a study of how similar the topics in high-rated essays written by students on a particular subject are to the topics in low-rated essays written by different students on the same subject.

Perhaps the most striking difference is that in the poorer essays a much higher percentage of the sentence topics were pronouns. Specifically, many of them were the personal pronouns *I*, *you*, and *we*. The essays had very few topics referring to nonpersonal things or to ideas.

This finding is true of many of the essays that I read every year, especially of those written in basic or remedial classes or toward the beginning of regular classes. Many of these essays rarely have topics other than *I*, *you*, and *we*. And when they do, these other topics are often words such as *one* and *people*.

For example, when I asked some of my students to evaluate the changes in people's behavior as those people moved from one social situation to another, I received essays with sentences such as these:

> As for myself, I try to—or think I do—behave the same wherever I am.
>
> When I am with a group of friends I tend to go along with the group and follow the general opinion of what to do next, but if I am with just one friend, I tend to do whatever I or my friend wants to do.
>
> When we don't change our behavior from one group to another group, some of the group may not like you for what you are.

On the other hand, in the better essays, there were not nearly so many pronouns as topics. Instead, there were more nouns referring to objects and to concepts such as honesty and hypocrisy. These writers often focused on ideas.

All this suggests that the writers of the poorer essays focused their work in a limited way. They focused mainly on themselves and their own experiences or on the experiences of those they took to be their readers. This is not necessarily bad; many writers produce excellent personal essays by focusing on themselves and on their experiences.

However, this kind of topicalization practice can be bad when it occurs as a response to an assignment that calls for a widely applicable point. And it can be bad when it is a sign of writers not thinking about others' experiences, others' perceptions, the wider implications of their own experiences, the more general concepts and issues that their experiences relate to, and the reasons why others should even bother to take their writing seriously. Such topicalization practices often reveal writers who think only of themselves. These writers neither state nor imply a more general point that others might wish to consider.

Why some writers focus only on themselves is difficult to explain. Some might do so because it is easier. One of my students introduced his essay on changes in people's behavior as follows:

> Why do we act differently in front of different people and does such an attitude have any consequences? These questions are hard to answer in a general sense; however, I will answer on my own behalf.

Other writers might focus in this way because they are not fully capable of abstract thought. They do not tend to think in terms of ideas such as hypocrisy and consistency; they see only people, primarily themselves and their friends, acting in certain ways. If this explanation is correct, it would have some frightening implications, since people who cannot think in terms of abstract ideas probably can do little real critical thinking.

My advice, then, is that if you find yourself topicalizing words such as *I, you,* and *we* often in an essay, you probably should distance yourself from your essay a little and consider whether you are focusing widely enough. You might have presented a too narrow set of focal points. You might have to enlarge the set of what you write about to include more general issues and abstract ideas.

Exercise Three

Examine each of the following sentences with a personal topic and state what more widely applicable point you could make about essentially the same subject matter.

For example, if you were to read *I always feel uneasy when I have to meet several people for the first time,* you could come up with a more general statement by changing the topic and any words that refer back to it: *Many people feel uneasy when they have to meet several others for the first time.*

1. I try to watch what I say, but usually my big mouth gets me into trouble.
2. As I entered the funeral home, I felt intense grief, but I could think of nothing to say to the relatives of the deceased.
3. We were so busy trying to impress those girls that we did not realize our jokes were hurting Bob's feelings.
4. I started talking about him without realizing that he could hear everything I said.
5. When I am with the guys I act rowdy and rough, but when I go out on a date I am much more courteous.

TOPICS: ABSTRACT AND GENERAL, CONCRETE AND SPECIFIC

I must immediately qualify the advice I just gave because many students have no trouble at all avoiding personal pronouns as topics. In fact, they have the opposite problem from the one I just described. They write only about abstract ideas.

Such prose can be criticized in many ways. First, it can be difficult to read. Often writers produce sentences with abstractions as their topics by taking meanings that would ordinarily be expressed with verbs (for example, *analyze*) and expressing them as nouns (*analysis*). This process is called *nominalizing*, since it involves making a noun out of a verb. And that noun often names an abstraction. Instead of writing *They analyzed the results*, writers with a tendency to nominalization produce *An analysis of the results was performed by them*.

This second sentence may not seem much more difficult to read than the first, largely because it is isolated and contains only one nominalization. But it is more difficult to understand and remember because it has more than twice the number of words that the first does and because it disrupts a correspondence between meaning and sentence structure that makes prose readable. This correspondence is between the agent (doer) in a sentence and the grammatical subject, between the action and the grammatical verb, and between the goal or receiver of the action and the direct object.

In *They analyzed the results*, the agents are referred to in the grammatical subject, *They*. The action is referred to in the verb, *analyzed*. And the goal of the activity is referred to in the direct object, *results*. Such a pattern of correspondences provides a useful touchstone for readability in sentences.

On the other hand, in *An analysis of the results was performed by them*, the agent appears not in the subject but in a prepositional phrase at the end of the sentence. The action is expressed not in the verb but is absorbed into the nominalization *analysis*, which serves as the subject. Therefore, what was a fairly energetic verb in the first sentence (*analyzed*) is replaced by a fairly weak one in the second (*was performed*). Finally, the goal of the activity appears not in the direct object but in a prepositional phrase attached to the subject. The agent, action, and goal do not appear where we expect them to. The agent, for example, appears far from where we expect it to and in a construction (a prepositional phrase) that we do not expect. Also, it is worth noting that this expression of meanings demands a passive verb. Since this sentence seriously disrupts the correspondences described above, and since it introduces a passive verb, it is more difficult to read than the first. One must think twice, therefore, before topicalizing many abstract nominalizations.

Exercise Four

Each of the following sentences topicalizes an abstract nominalization. Revise each so that it topicalizes the actual agent. For example, you could revise *All of the examinations of courses proposed for the interim period were carried out by the Educational Policy Committee* to *The Educational Policy Committee examined the courses proposed for the interim period*. In some cases, you might have to invent a plausible agent.

1. An investigation of the number of agencies willing to provide grant money for a computer laboratory was carried out by the *ad hoc* committee on computers.
2. The decision to require additional evaluations of the new courses has been made by the provost.
3. Their hope is to complete the bicycle race in less than two weeks.
4. Little justification for using three novels in the composition course was offered by the new instructors.
5. A need to come to meetings with better preparation has often been exhibited by them.
6. The discovery that he was now on a committee that had to produce several documents per semester was made by Dale.
7. A close examination of the reasons given by them for his failure on the preliminary test was made by him.
8. Our expectation is that you will be able to do an excellent job in that advanced course.
9. A review of the graduation requirements for those in the education program has been carried out.
10. Determination to defeat the intramural football champions has been expressed.

The second reason why prose in which many abstractions are topicalized can be criticized is that if we begin to depend on such abstractions, they can distort our thinking and can end up controlling us to some extent. For example, if we grow accustomed to sentences such as *True devotion requires that all followers send in a $50 donation* or *Proper stewardship demands that there can be only one response to the ecological crisis*, we might begin to lose track of some important things. Can devotion demand? Or stewardship indicate? No. These abstract concepts are based on relationships that we perceive or try to cultivate among values, authorities, people, and objects. Standing behind the two example sentences are real people trying for various reasons to do things to other people or to objects. But such facts are obscured when we write that "devotion requires" or "stewardship demands." And the more such facts are obscured, the more likely it is that we will forget about them and become slaves to the abstractions that dominate our discourse.

The third reason to criticize prose in which many abstractions are topicalized is that it reveals none of its author's personality. It seems to have no identifiable voice because it demonstrates so little commitment. Most people would call such prose dull, lifeless, and impersonal.

Thus I must balance my earlier advice about considering whether you should topicalize more abstract ideas and fewer personal pronouns. Most prose needs some abstract and general sentence topics, especially at beginnings and ends of paragraphs and of longer subunits. These topics help make the points that will appeal to more people than the author and those that have had experiences similar to the author's. Also, these topics can convey fine distinctions in thought as well as very specialized and technical ideas. But these topics should be introduced or followed by more concrete, specific, and personal topics. These will bring the widely applicable points to life.

For example, in an essay about changes in people's behavior, you might choose to start with a general point about an abstract concept such as hypocrisy. Then you might go on to support this claim with several sentences that make concrete points about specific persons acting hypocritically. And you could conclude with a sentence that again topicalizes an abstraction such as hypocrisy or consistency.

To understand better why such a balance is desirable, we should take a closer look at the meanings of *abstract, general, concrete,* and *specific.*

Abstract and *concrete* are usually defined together or in terms of each other. The abstract is that which exists only in our minds, that which we cannot know through our senses. It includes qualities, relationships, conditions, ideas, theories, states of being, fields of inquiry, and the like. We cannot know a quality such as consistency directly through our senses; we can only see or hear about people acting in ways that we come to label consistent.

On the other hand, the concrete we can know directly through our senses. We can touch sand on the beach, smell salt water, and see driftwood. For our purposes, we can say that things are either abstract or concrete; we will not debate whether there are degrees of concreteness.

The terms *general* and *specific* are also usually defined together. As words become more general, they refer to more things; as they become more specific, they refer to fewer. The most specific words refer to only one thing. Words are not either general or specific; they are more or less general or specific relative to other words. For example, *footwear* is more general than *shoes*, *shoes* is more general than *athletic shoes*, and *athletic shoes* is more general than *running shoes*. Or to look at it from the other side, my tattered Nike Elite® running shoes are more specific than all other Nike® running shoes.

Earlier I wrote that as you select sentence topics, you should seek an effective balance between abstract and more general topics and concrete and more specific topics. I wrote this because I believe that prose with only concrete and very specific or personal topics will usually lead to points or implications that only a limited number of people will understand, take seriously, and see the importance of. Readers can find such prose focused so specifically that they are unable to find a general point to draw from it. At the same time, I believe that prose with only abstract and general topics can seem rather remote. Readers can find it focused so broadly that they think its points do not apply to them.

But there is another, very important reason for balancing abstract and general topics with concrete and specific ones. This reason is that these different kinds of words appeal to different faculties in us. Abstract and general terms appeal to our reason, to our intellect. We think about them; we do not become emotional about them.

For example, here is Plato writing in *The Republic* about temperance:

> Temperance is not like courage and wisdom, which make the state wise and brave by residing each in one particular part. Temperance works in a different way; it extends throughout the whole gamut of the state, producing a consonance of all its elements from the weakest to the strongest as measured by any standard you like to take—wisdom, bodily strength, numbers, or wealth.
>
> (Translated by Francis MacDonald Cornford, pp. 125–126)

Three topics appear in this passage: *Temperance*, *Temperance*, and *it*. Each of these refers to the abstract quality of temperance. It is very difficult for me to imagine anyone's emotions being deeply stirred by this passage. Rather, I believe that it appeals to our reason. We think about what the terms mean, try to follow and evaluate the argument, and then consider the consequences of the argument if it is valid. If those consequences please us, we may feel some pleasure. Or if they displease us, we may feel some fear or irritation. But the passage works first and most thoroughly on our reasoning abilities.

On the other hand, concrete and specific words appeal to our emotions. I will probably never forget the scripts for some of the movies that I saw while taking drivers' education classes. These movies were intended to motivate us to drive carefully. Some of the script writers really knew how to move our emotions, specifically our fear and revulsion. They wrote about a specific man, gave us his name, described his leaving home in Toledo on a July day in a new Ford to drive to Cedar Point Amusement Park. On the way there he had a terrible accident. Then the writers focused on his face, shredded by the glass of the windshield; on his left arm lying detached from his body in the median; and on his broken right leg with its thigh bone protruding through the rent material of his pants. Later the writers focused on how specific members of the man's family reacted to this accident.

Of course, these writers could use music and images on film as well as words in appealing to more than one of our senses, a technique that in itself usually moves the emotions. But you can probably guess how we reacted. Some of us sweated, some vomited, some fainted. After one such movie, I was so scared that I did not ride my bike home on the street; I rode home on the sidewalk and walked my bike across intersections.

I hope that my point is clear: I was never very scared after hearing generalizations about how many people die in traffic accidents each year. Nor was I very scared when I heard about abstractions such as drunk driving, reckless driving, or defensive driving. I was, however, scared when a writer wrote about something terrible happening to one man and when the writer and the film director focused my attention on aspects of the tragedy.

In my terror I was not thinking very carefully or clearly. And generally, I suspect, as our emotions are moved more intensely, it is more difficult for us to use our reason. We have all probably had the experience of discovering how hard it is to think clearly when we are upset or ecstatic. At the same time, the more our rational abilities are engaged, the more difficult it is for our emotions to be moved. Try to get those in the flow of solving an intricate and intriguing calculus problem to drop it and suddenly feel an emotion.

Once you know all this, you have some powerful tools to use in your writing. You can work primarily on your readers' intellects. You can work primarily on their emotions. Or you can take my earlier advice and work on both their intellects and their emotions. In other words, you can use abstract and general topics for some sentences and concrete and specific topics for others.

If you follow this advice, you will be closer to appealing to people in their wholeness. And that is usually effective. If you appeal only to people's rational abilities, they might accept your claims but feel little force in them. They might think without acting. On the other hand, if you appeal only to people's emotions, they might react to your writing very strongly but not evaluate it and what it could lead to carefully enough. They might act without thinking.

I can only guess, but my guess is that there are more purely emotional appeals than purely intellectual appeals in what we read from day to day. I think most immediately of some of the prose on both sides of the abortion issue. Some of the pro-life materials appeal to only our emotions as the materials center on actions taken on fetuses. And some of the pro-choice materials appeal to only our emotions as these materials center on actions taken on or by women. In such a situation, people whose emotions are stirred little or not at all by actions on fetuses will simply dismiss the pro-life proposals. And people whose emotions are stirred little or not at all by actions on or by women will simply dismiss the pro-choice proposals. There is nothing but emotion to go on.

However, if you appeal to readers' rational abilities as well, you can build a fuller and stronger case. You have a good chance of getting readers to evaluate your claims, accept your claims, remember your claims, and act on your claims.

Exercise Five

Each of the following sentences topicalizes an abstract or general idea or quality. To support the idea or quality, add some sentences after each statement that topicalize more specific and concrete things.

For example, you could see a sentence such as *Honesty is indeed the best policy.* After this you could add sentences focusing on how a friend of yours plagiarized a paper, was accused of doing so by the instructor, and was led to more and more lies as she or he tried to cover up the initial deception.

1. Closed-mindedness is very difficult to cope with.
2. The phoniness in television evangelism is sickening.
3. Greed almost invariably leads to trouble.
4. Repressing emotions can be harmful.

5. Political posturing by world leaders can be dangerous.
6. Pride is the one trait that cannot be tolerated.
7. Constant punning can be annoying.
8. Humor helps teaching on any level.
9. Sarcasm does no one any good.
10. Kind words calm the angriest people.

TOPICS AND ETHICS, PART II

As a follow-up to our discussion of ethics in Chapter Two, I argue that writers have additional ethical responsibilities in choosing what to topicalize. To begin developing this claim, I quote what one of the boys in our neighborhood said after he tossed my model airplane onto the roof of our garage: "Bill, Bill, come into the backyard. Your airplane got stuck on the garage!" Note what he topicalized in his second sentence—*Your airplane*. He wanted me to focus on it, and not on him, the one who tossed it onto the roof. He did not say "I just tossed your airplane onto the garage roof."

What he did was precisely what my sons do when they inadvertently knock a piece of silverware onto the floor during meals. They say, "Oops. My fork just fell on the floor."

In both of these cases, speakers use topics to take the focus off themselves as agents and to put it on objects that are hard to blame and impossible to punish.

I certainly do not claim that these examples represent serious ethical issues. Nor would I claim that writers are manipulative each time they take the focus off a human agent. Sometimes they do so for good reasons.

Often I read in accident reports in newspapers something like, "The car left the road and smashed into a telephone pole, killing the driver." Here again, a writer takes the focus off a human agent, the driver, and puts it on an object, a car. The writer makes it seem as if the car willfully smashed itself and killed its human occupant. Sometimes cars do have mechanical problems that cause them to leave the road, or they skid on icy roads. And sometimes reporters do not know why a car left the road—they only know that it did. Thus they report what they know, not what they hypothesize.

Often, though, there is an obvious problem with the driver. But if writers were to describe an accident with a focus on the driver ("George P. Pulliam, who obviously had been drinking, drove his car off the road and directly into a telephone pole. He died in the collision."), they would probably be heaping unnecessary torment on the victim's grieving friends and relatives.

Having granted this, I want to alert you once again that as we choose topics we can decide to move within what Frederick Bowers calls a paradigm of increasing irresponsibility. For example, we can describe an incident in several different ways:

> We cracked your headlight with our baseball.
> Our baseball cracked your headlight.
> Your headlight was cracked by our baseball.
> Your headlight got cracked.
> Your headlight cracked.

As we move through these sentences, we see that in each successive form the true agents become increasingly obscured and that objects that cannot act on their own and are less and less connected to the true agents are brought into focus. And often those objects seem to be invested with agency. Of course, certain syntactical devices (such as the passive) also play a role here. But in each case the topic reveals what the writer wants his or her readers to focus on.

And as the focal point moves further from the true agent, and as the actions themselves move into the realm of deception and harm, we would have to say that writers are using topics unethically. What if a rental agent promised that he would make an apartment available to you for $500 a month but when you are ready to move in said, "Inflation pushed the price up"? What if a squad of soldiers forcibly removed all the civilians from their village, cut down the trees in and around the village, bulldozed and mined the land around the village, and later justified all these actions by saying, "Creating a sanitized belt demanded strong measures"? Does such a sentence seem unlikely to you? If it does, you should know that during the Vietnam War civilians who were killed by mistake were referred to as "regrettable by-products," that the destruction of a village could be called "pacification," and that an all-out invasion could be described as a "reinforced protective reaction strike." I also remind you of the last epigraph for this chapter, in which SS officers are quoted as topicalizing *the war* and not themselves.

Exercise Six

Explain why the writer of each of the following sentences probably topicalized as he or she did. Do you think that any of these apparent motives are unethical?

1. The mustard spilled all over my shirt.
2. Streamlining our department demands that your contract be terminated.
3. The plane veered off the runway, smashed into a row of lights, and burst into flames.
4. Building up a grade point average impressive enough to get me into medical school forced me to use some of my roommate's answers.
5. That bottle of paint thinner dropped and sent liquid all over the basement floor.
6. National security interests require that all phones in that district be tapped.
7. The picture window cracked.
8. The car went right through the gate.
9. Culturally biased questions have brought down some students' scores on nationally normed tests.
10. The spiraling national debt will necessitate a hike in taxes in the next two years.

TOPICALIZATION TECHNIQUES
AND PROCESSES

Everything that I have written about the first guideline presupposes that as we write we have choices about what to topicalize. It would be senseless for me to suggest that you should evaluate the words and phrases that could serve as topics of your sentences and pick the most appropriate one in context if only one element in each sentence could serve as its topic.

But as we saw at the beginning of Chapter Two, the English language offers us some choices about what to topicalize in each sentence. The word order of English is fairly rigid (most sentences move from subjects through verbs to objects or complements), but still the language provides us with some syntactic devices to move words and phrases around in sentences.

To a certain extent, therefore, we can shift different elements into positions associated with topics (early positions and positions associated with the grammatical subject). And in some cases we can use syntactic devices to call special attention to the words or phrases that we topicalize.

Of course, there are limits to the amount and kind of shifting that we can do. Sometimes we might have good reasons to want to topicalize certain words, but the only way to do so would produce a clumsy or unnatural sentence. For example; when earlier in this chapter I was discussing some evidence that readers tend to assume that a topic will carry over from one sentence to the next, I wrote the sentence "We make these associations readily." Actually, when I was working on that sentence, I wanted to get *these associations* into the topic, since they were more closely related to material I had just written than was *We*. But to do so, I would have had to write something like *But making these associations is hesitated over by no one.* And that sentence I judged too clumsy to use.

Thus you will have to use the devices I describe next with care. They can be used to topicalize appropriately and to call special attention to topics if the situation warrants it. But sometimes they can lead to awkward forms. If you learn them, practice them, and use them with discretion, you should increase your control over your style and, in turn, improve the clarity of your prose.

What follows, then, is a list of techniques for rearranging elements from what might be considered the normal order within a sentence. Some of these we can use to move words and phrases into a topic position. One or two of these we can use to call special attention to our topics. Moreover, most of these are associated with special rhetorical functions within essays. In many cases I will be working with the following sentence to produce examples: *Alma typed the manuscript.*

Topicalizers

The easiest place to start is with some words and phrases called *topicalizers*. Typical topicalizers are *concerning, as for, speaking of, with regard to, with reference to, with respect to, in the matter of, when it comes to,* and *as far as* _____ *is concerned.* These are probably more common in speech, but they appear in writing as well.

When they appear, they are normally used to pick out a word or phrase in a sentence and to move it to the beginning. A pronoun typically appears where the word or phrase originally did. For example, with *Alma typed the manuscript,* I could use the topicalizer *as for* to move *the manuscript* to the beginning of the sentence. The pronoun *it* would then appear where *the manuscript* did. Thus:

> As for the manuscript, Alma typed it.

If I wanted *Alma* to remain the topic of the sentence and also wanted to call special attention to her, I could use a topicalizer to do so:

> As for Alma, she typed the manuscript.

Writers use topicalizers to fulfill some special functions in essays. In general, they use them when the situation warrants that a fairly large amount of attention be drawn to the topic.

For instance, writers often use topicalizers to call attention to topics that are related to ones that they have been commenting on but that have not yet appeared themselves. In such cases, writers can probably assume that their readers are wondering when they will present a certain topic, and when they do so, they present it with the mild flourish of a topicalizer.

For example, Peter Trudgill details ways in which dialects in Great Britain differ from one another. He gives examples of differences in vocabulary and goes on to describe differences in syntax. Then he comes to sounds, or accent. He introduces this concept with a topicalizer:

> As far as accent is concerned, the situation is slightly different. . . .
>
> (*Sociolinguistics: An Introduction*, p. 41)

Perhaps more often, writers use topicalizers to mark changes in topics. They frequently do so with topics that they have mentioned earlier and that they now wish to reintroduce and expand upon, often in a new light.

For example, Cynthia Ozick claims that what ancient Greek culture lacked was metaphor. She immediately imagines readers saying, "What about myths? What about the utterances of the oracle at Delphi? Weren't those metaphoric?" She mentions these objections and proceeds to argue that Greek myths were not metaphoric. Then she comes back to the topic of the Delphic utterances, which she reintroduces with a topicalizer:

As for the Delphic riddles: they were recipes, not standards.

("The Moral Necessity of Metaphor,"
Harper's Magazine, May, 1986, p. 65)

And just as often, probably, writers use topicalizers to set up contrasts between one topic and another. Sometimes the contrast is only a potential one. Lewis Thomas uses a topicalizer in this way immediately after he asserts that our genetic material may have come from many different sources in nature:

> As for me, I am grateful for differentiation and speciation, but I cannot feel as separate an entity as I did a few years ago, before I was told these things, nor, I should think, can anyone else.

("The Lives of a Cell," *The Lives of a Cell*, p. 3)

It is as if Thomas writes, "I can speak only for myself now, and my view might contrast with others' views, although it probably should not."

Sometimes, however, the contrast is actual and explicit; it is the point of the section. The last part of Joshua 24:15 uses a topicalizer in this way:

> And if it is disagreeable in your sight to serve the Lord, choose for yourselves today whom you will serve: whether the gods which your fathers served which were beyond the River, or the gods of the Amorites in whose land you are living; but as for me and my house, we will serve the Lord.

(American Standard Version)

Finally, writers often add yet another wrinkle by setting up a contrast to trivialize, negate, or dismiss a topic:

> Majors in our department have issued two complaints against us professors. The first, we admit, has some validity. As for the second, however, it is utter nonsense.

Reversals

With some verbs (forms of *to be*, and verbs such as *lie, rest, sit, hover*, and *stand*), we can reverse the position or identity of subjects and complements. We would do so, of course, if we wanted what would ordinarily be expressed in the complement in the topic.

For example, in a passage in which I am topicalizing references to my friend Wayne, I would not write *The dean of the Graduate School of*

Business is Wayne but *Wayne is the dean of the Graduate School of Business.* Or in a passage in which I am focusing on a controversy between students and administrators over the management of some stocks, I would not write *The problem of what to do with the students' petition for disinvestment lies at the very heart of the controversy* but *At the very heart of the controversy lies the problem of what to do with the students' petition for disinvestment.*

Writers often use reversals to connect the topic of a sentence to what has preceded it. For instance, Stephen Jay Gould writes about how difficult it is for an evolutionist to explain perfection in animals. He then moves on to discuss repeated perfection in a number of unrelated animals. He does not cast his sentence thus:

> Repeated perfection by very different animals is the only thing more difficult to explain than perfection.

This sentence misses the chance to express in its topic something nearly identical to what has just been expressed. So Gould produces the reverse of my example:

> The only thing more difficult to explain than perfection is repeated perfection by very different animals.
>
> ("Double Trouble," *The Panda's Thumb,* p. 37)

The Passive

We can reverse the position of subject and object by changing transitive verbs from the active to the passive voice. In fact, many linguists believe that the passive occurs in languages primarily to let speakers and writers topicalize what would normally be the indirect or direct object of the sentence. To refer to the sample sentence again, we see that with a passive we can change *Alma typed the manuscript* to *The manuscript was typed by Alma.*

Many of my students say that they have been told by one teacher or another never to use passive verbs. Teachers have some good reasons for saying this.

Passives almost always lead to longer sentences than corresponding active verbs do. They are often harder to read, since they frustrate our reading strategy of searching in each sentence for the agent, the action, and the goal of the action, in that order. Passives move the goal of the action to the beginning of a sentence and the agent to the end. And sometimes references to the agent are omitted altogether (*The manuscript was typed*).

With such omissions, it can be impossible to figure out who did or is doing something. Such is true of the first official Soviet statement about the nuclear accident at Chernobyl:

> An accident has taken place at the Chernobyl power station, and one of the reactors was damaged. Measures are being taken to eliminate the consequences of the accident. Those affected by it are being given assistance. A government commission has been set up.

Such omissions can have ethical implications when those at fault in an illegal or unscrupulous action describe the action with a passive and omit references to themselves as the agents: *The reports that show gross mismanagement of college funds have been mislaid.*

For all these reasons, we are wise to be cautious about passives. But we should not take an oath to avoid them, since passives have important functions for maintaining or establishing topics. However, we must justify their use and employ them with care.

If we use passives to topicalize properly, that gain will offset the losses incurred with greater sentence length and with the order of goals before agents. As we have seen, we topicalize properly when we keep consecutive sentence topics similar or identical.

John le Carré uses a passive to do this. He focuses on a cable offering Alastair, an actor, a choice movie part:

> It [the cable] had come up to the farmhouse on a Lambretta at ten that morning; it had been brought down to the beach by Willy and Pauly, who had been having a late lie-in. It offered what it styled "possibility major film part." . . .

> (*The Little Drummer Girl*, p. 56)

Le Carré could have written the second independent clause in the active voice: *Willy and Pauly brought the cable down to the beach.* But this clause focuses on Willy and Pauly and not on the cable, which is the focal point for several clauses in a row.

The passive is also a good choice when the agent is either obvious or unimportant. Such elements do not make good candidates for sentence topics, since we should not write about the obvious or unimportant. Ordinarily one says that "I was born" on a certain date, not that "My mother gave birth to me."

Peter Trudgill uses a passive for this purpose:

An experiment was carried out in the USA in which a number of people acting as judges were asked to listen to tape recordings of two different sets of speakers.

(Sociolinguistics: An Introduction, p. 57)

What is important here is the experiment (one to check people's intuitions about the races of speakers recorded on tape) and its results, not those who performed the experiment. This might not always be true. It might not, for instance, if the research team has a record of shoddy experiments. But in this case the passive is justified in order to topicalize *An experiment*. This sentence would have an inappropriate topic if it began with *Some researchers in the USA*. Trudgill, in fact, in keeping with the view that a good experiment could be repeated with the same results by other researchers, deletes the phrase that could be included after *carried out: by some researchers*.

Fronting

In some sentences, we can make an element topical simply by moving it to the beginning of the sentence. We could do this with our sample sentence, changing *Alma typed the manuscript* into *The manuscript Alma typed*. We can do this with single words:

He had brains.
Brains he had.

Or with phrases:

She cared very deeply about wildlife refuges.
About wildlife refuges she cared very deeply.

Or even with clauses:

He knew that the Birkebeiner was a long race.
That the Birkebeiner was a long race he knew.

Writers use this technique in some interesting ways. One of these is to mark important connections between topics and preceding material. For example, about two-thirds of the way through an essay entitled "Cry for Cambodia," Edward E. Ericson, Jr., fronts and topicalizes a long phrase:

Of the suffering of the Cambodian people we seldom have reason to think.

(*The Reformed Journal*, February, 1986, p. 3)

Before this sentence, he documents many of the sufferings of the Cambodian people. And after this sentence he offers some reasons why we rarely think of the Cambodians' suffering. In this sentence, then, Ericson fronts some material to produce a topic that captures the essence of earlier parts of the essay. He is thus also able to produce a comment that introduces the substance of the latter portions of his essay.

Fronted elements are perhaps even more commonly used when two or more items have been brought up and are then contrasted with each other. A famous pair of fronts in the Bible works this way:

Just as it is written, "Jacob I loved, but Esau I hated."

(Romans 9:13, ASV)

Dickens also uses fronts in this way in some of Mrs. Micawber's speech:

"We came," repeated Mrs. Micawber, "and saw the Medway. My opinion of the coal trade on that river, is that it may require talent, but that it certainly requires capital. Talent, Mr. Micawber has; capital, Mr. Micawber has not."

(*David Copperfield*, p. 266)

Exercise Seven

Using material that you create, write sentences that imitate the structure of each sentence in the following clusters. You may use some of the words (for example, topicalizers) that are used here. For instance, consider the following three sentences:

The boys spilled the thinner and the motor oil on the garage floor. The thinner will evaporate without a trace. As for the oil, it will leave a dark stain.

You could imitate these structures by writing *She read a short story and a poem. The story did not affect her. As for the poem, it moved her deeply.*

1. John and Dave are two of my close friends. John I saw over the Memorial Day weekend. As for Dave, I have not seen him in two years.
2. We take our opponents fairly seriously. They have an undeniably potent offense. But as for their defense, it is almost nonexistent.
3. To this date, the negotiations have been stalled for three weeks. Hovering over the deadlock is the issue of maternity leave.
4. The research team is stumped by the origin of the word *astimagutus*. Just as perplexing is the cause of the Minor Vowel Shift.
5. Some people complain that "America the Beautiful" is difficult to sing. But even more difficult to sing is "The Star-Spangled Banner."
6. In preparation for Summerfest, all of the streets have been roped off. In addition, some stages for the performing arts have been set up.
7. When the police arrived on the scene, they discovered that all of the widow's jewels had been stolen. But none of her municipal bonds had been touched.
8. We looked at two used cars last week. The first my wife thought was too small. And the second my sons thought was too old.
9. We all knew that she spent many hours translating poetry. But of this work she seldom spoke.
10. That job required intelligence and courage. Intelligence he has. Courage he lacks.

Exercise Eight

Change the last sentence in each of the following clusters according to the instructions that follow in parentheses. For example, you might see a sentence such as *He examined the ruins.* And you could be asked to reverse the positions of subject and object by making the verb passive. Thus you would write *The ruins were examined by him.*

1. She told us that she had to write a short article and a review essay. The article she was nearly finished with. However, she had not even started the review essay. (Begin the sentence with the topicalizer *As for*, topicalizing *the review essay*.)
2. The principal threatened to suspend those students for a week and to bar them from taking exams. The first threat he has the power to carry out. He does not have the authority to carry out the second. (Begin the sentence with *As for*, topicalizing *the second*.)

905378

3. Learning how to ski is easy. Learning how to get on the chairlifts is not so easy. (Reverse the positions of the full subject and the complement.)
4. They have been debating that issue all semester. The question about political responsibility is what lies at the heart of the debate. (Reverse the positions of the full subject and complement.)
5. John moved from college into a very fulfilling job. The director of personnel for a large firm in Ohio is John. (Reverse the positions of the full subject and complement; use any pronouns that you think are necessary.)
6. The window had been smashed. And someone had sprayed paint on the walls. (Topicalize *paint* by changing the verb to the passive voice; omit any elements that you think are unnecessary.)
7. The goldfish was not in its tank. The cat had eaten it. (Topicalize *it* by changing the verb to the passive voice.)
8. Broca and le Bon are interested in artificial intelligence. A prestigious research grant was won by them last year. (Change *them* to *they* and topicalize it, changing the verb to the active voice.)
9. Marathons he has always excelled in. He has never done well in ten kilometer races. (Front *ten kilometer races.*)
10. Late in her life she became acutely aware of the suffering of the homeless in the big cities. She writes with great intensity about this suffering. (Front *about this suffering.*)

Exercise Nine

In each of the following short paragraphs, one sentence is not topicalized as it should be. Find these sentences and revise them so that they have appropriate topics in context.

For example, consider the following short paragraph:

> Swimmer's itch has afflicted many people this summer. Bacteria carried by snails cause it. And it is spread from lake to lake by ducks who eat the snails and excrete the bacteria.

Here the second sentence is not topicalized properly. It topicalizes *Bacteria*, while the other two sentences topicalize *Swimmer's itch* or a reference to swimmer's itch. The second sentence should be revised to read as follows: *It is caused by bacteria carried by snails.*

1. Three problems have plagued the program to revitalize the downtown area. The first is that some of those who pledged to support the

program have not fulfilled their pledges. The second is that cost overruns have pushed the price far higher than anyone had imagined. And the concurrent successful development of three large malls in the suburbs is the third problem.

2. As advertised, the position demands intelligence, energy, and tact. Intelligence he has. And energy he has in abundance. But he completely lacks tact.

3. Currently, Ed is our representative on the academic council. He is also a member of the Academic Standards Committee. Finally, the Chair of our department is Ed.

4. Charlotte has investigated several topics in seventeenth-century English poetry. She has examined how the poets used allusions to plants— some harmless and some poisonous—to reinforce themes. She has explored how women are depicted in the love poems of the period. And recently some of Shakespeare's allusions have been studied by her.

5. The administrative offices had been broken into and ransacked. All the file cabinets had been pried open, and file folders were strewn all over the floor. Whoever broke in had slashed the portraits of former presidents of the university. The desks had been overturned. And all the walls had been spray-painted with at least a dozen colors of paint.

6. We have only begun to understand the complexities of human language. And programming computers to acquire language as human children do is a research task just as challenging as this.

TO REVIEW:
CHOOSING SENTENCE TOPICS

As we have seen, English does not allow us unrestricted freedom to move elements around in sentences to topicalize as we might wish. But it does provide us with enough means so that we have a good deal of flexibility in what we can topicalize. The essence of the first guideline is that we should use these means to topicalize in one sentence an element or elements that are identical to, similar to, closely related to, or part of the same scenario or field of meaning as that of earlier topics or comments in that portion of an essay. As we shall see in more detail in Chapter Seven, doing this will contribute significantly to the clarity and coherence of your prose.

FURTHER READING

Bosmajian, H. (1986). "Dehumanizing People and Euphemizing War," *The Christian Century*, 5 December 1984.

Bowers, F. (1971). "Meaning and Sentence Structure," *English Quarterly, 4,* 5-12.

Brown, G., and G. Yule (1983). "Topic and the Representation of Discourse Content," *Discourse Analysis.* Cambridge: Cambridge University Press.

Stotsky, S. (1986). "On Learning to Write About Ideas," *College Composition and Communication, 37,* 276-293.

Van Dijk, T. A., and W. Kintsch (1983). "Local Coherence Strategies," *Strategies of Discourse Comprehension.* Orlando: Academic Press, Inc.

Williams, J. M. (1980). "Non-linguistic Linguistics and the Teaching of Style," *Language and Style, 13,* 24-40.

Williams, J. M. (1985). "The Grammar of Coherence," *Style: Ten Lessons in Clarity and Grace* (2nd ed.). Glenview, IL: Scott, Foresman.

CHAPTER

4

Expressing Topics in Appropriate Forms and Places

Point of view, perspective, position, line of sight—angle is everything.
—William H. Gass, "Emerson and the Essay,"
Habitations of the Word

Our very recognition of complexity depends upon the clarity of our vision of the elements which go to make it up.
—Wayne C. Booth, *The Rhetoric of Fiction,*
First Edition

"Begin at the beginning," the King said, very gravely, "and go on till you come to the end: then stop."

—Lewis Carroll, *Alice's Adventures in Wonderland*

We all remember how in school examinations we sometimes shoveled in words, the longer the better, to cover up a complete lack of knowledge about a given question.
—Stuart Chase, *The Tyranny of Words*

Having examined some techniques that we can use to rearrange elements in a sentence in order to topicalize properly, we can now move to the second guideline for clear and coherent writing.

THE SECOND GUIDELINE

The second guideline is as follows: In general, make it as easy as possible for readers to identify your sentence topics.

Earlier I wrote that topics often appear early in sentences, are identical to the first noun or noun phrase in a sentence, and correspond to the grammatical subject. All these characteristics—but particularly the correspondence between topic and subject—make it quite easy for readers to establish early in a sentence what it will be about.

But sometimes the topic and the subject do not correspond. And if we explore some of the reasons why they do not, we will learn more about how to make topics easily identifiable for readers. A good way to accomplish all this is to look at some common patterns of elements for the early part of sentences. I will describe these patterns in terms of the first element (FE) in a sentence (which can include more than one word if the words form a phrase or clause functioning within another grammatical structure), the grammatical subject of the independent clause (S), and the topic (T).

Pattern Number One

In this pattern, the first element, the subject, and the topic are all the same (FE=S=T). For example:

FE, S, T

Cross-country skiing is both strenuous and very relaxing.

Pattern Number Two

In this pattern, the subject and the topic are identical, but they do not correspond to the first element (FE; S=T). For example:

FE   S, T

In the second place, cross-country skiing is both strenuous and very relaxing.

Pattern Number Three

In this pattern, the first element and the subject are the same, but they are different from the topic (FE=S; T). For instance:

FE,S   T

It is undeniably the case that cross-country skiing is both strenuous and very relaxing.

This kind of sentence usually results when a writer uses an introductory *it* or *there*. When these words are used in this way, they are called expletives or even dummy subjects (since they carry no real information). Many linguists, though, would say that they fill the slot of the grammatical subject of the main clause. The topic almost always appears later, as the subject of a subordinate clause.

Pattern Number Four

In this kind of sentence, the first element and the topic are the same or nearly the same, but they are different from the subject (FE=T; S). Here the introductory clause has to be examined within the context of the following clause. For example,

FE, T   S

When it comes to cross-country skiing, we can say that it is both strenuous and very relaxing.   Or:

FE, T   S

When all aspects of cross-country skiing are examined, it becomes clear that it is both strenuous and very relaxing.

Pattern Number Five

In this pattern, the first element, the subject, and the topic all differ from one another (FE; S; T). One example follows:

      FE   S   T

Actually, I am amazed that cross-country skiing is both strenuous and very relaxing.

Exercise One

In each of the following sentences, identify the first element, the subject, and the topic. For example, in *Frankly, it is clear that your case is weak*, the first element is *Frankly*, the subject (or the expletive in the subject slot) is *it*, and the topic is *your case*.

1. The members of that group claim that the world will end in a nuclear holocaust.
2. On the other hand, trying to hike to Ptarmigan Peak in one day might work out.
3. In the summer, he raises corn and soybeans on the ten-acre plot behind his house.
4. It was certainly the case that she had served the community as well as anyone had.
5. Finally, I must add that three tuition waivers are still available for next year.
6. When it comes to the underlying motivation of that generation, we can say virtually nothing.
7. In addition, the committee is happy to report that all the sabbatical proposals have been granted.
8. The town of Ispheming has an interesting history.
9. Unfortunately, the city commission voted to table that motion.
10. We are certain that the board of trustees will support that petition.

Exercise Two

Identify which of the five sentence patterns is exemplified in each of the following. For example, *Frankly, it is clear that your case is weak* is a Pattern Five sentence.

1. Moreover, Gary is working on a novel for children.
2. With regard to the history of that proposal to the faculty, we can say virtually nothing.
3. Lionel used a metaphor centering on seepage from a swamp to describe passages in time.
4. It seems unlikely that she will be back from Amsterdam in time to attend the honors convocation.
5. Surprisingly, there are only two things they are afraid of.
6. On the other hand, Steve will be moving out of his office near the end of August.
7. It is clear that you do not wish to be considered for the position of editor.
8. Marian is working on an essay about how women make ethical decisions.
9. Third, the hospital is searching for a heart donor.
10. Consequently, there are now several questions in the air about how to start that program up again.

METADISCOURSE

Pattern-five sentences usually appear when writers use at least two kinds of metadiscourse to begin sentences. One kind appears as the first element, and an element or elements of another appear as the grammatical subject.

Metadiscourse is language that does not appear in topics, does not add information about topics, and therefore does not expand the information about the overall subject of a passage. Therefore, most essays have at least two levels of language. One is the primary level, the level of topical material; on this level writers use topics and comments to convey information about states of affairs in the world. This is the kind of material that we have been concerned with so far. On the other level, the level of metadiscourse, writers do not convey information about the world but direct readers how to read, react to, and recall that information.

With metadiscourse, writers can fulfill many directing functions. It is not always easy to distinguish these functions or to say that one kind of metadiscourse fulfills one and only one function at all times. But it will help us implement Guideline Two better if we examine several kinds of metadiscourse in discrete groups.

Many examples of metadiscourse are best called connectives. They show how parts of passages are connected to each other. Some of these show sequences (*first, in the second place, finally*). Others show relationships of logic (*however, therefore*) or of time (*at the same time*). And others are reminders about topical material presented earlier in essays (*As I noted in the introduction*), statements about what material one is about to present (*What I wish to discuss now are*), and announcements of material that will appear later (*As we shall see in the next section*).

With a second kind of metadiscourse, writers let their readers know what specific action they are performing at a particular point in their essays. When we write, we perform actions such as introducing, claiming, promising, exemplifying, and concluding. And sometimes we tell our readers exactly what we are doing. We use phrases and clauses such as *to introduce this section, I claim that, I promise that, to give an example of this*, and *I note in conclusion that*. We can call examples of this kind of metadiscourse action markers.

Another kind of metadiscourse we use to show how we judge the probability or truth of the topical material we convey. The best name for these elements is perhaps unfamiliar to you: modality markers.

Some modality markers we use to hedge our statements (*perhaps, it is possible that*). We signal some doubt or tentativeness. Often we do this by indicating to what degree we think something is true (*to a certain degree*). Other modality markers we use to stress what we believe is true or what we wish our readers to think we take as true (*it is clear that, I note without reservation that, there can be no doubt that*). And still other modality markers we use to indicate in which personal or institutional framework we think something is true (*in Heisenberg's view, according to the conservative view of things*).

Closely related to these, but functioning slightly differently, are narrators. With them we let our readers know who said or wrote something. For them to be narrators and not modality markers, the probability or truth of topical material should not be at issue. In this category are elements such as *according to Tom, The chairman announced that*, and *Mary Ann pointed out that*.

Still another kind of metadiscourse allows us to reveal our actual or feigned attitudes toward topical material. We can indicate how important we think it is (*what's most important is*), how interesting we think it is (*more interesting still is the idea that*), and how it affects us emotionally (*I am alarmed to note that*).

Finally, there is a kind of metadiscourse best labeled commentary. When we use it, we address readers directly and appear to draw them into a conversation with us. We can comment on their probable reactions to topical material (*most of you will welcome the idea that*). We can recommend to them how to read our essays (*you might wish to skim this section first*). And we can let them know what to expect (*You will probably find the introductory material deceptively easy*).

In sum, there are at least six kinds of metadiscourse: connectives, action markers, modality markers, narrators, attitude markers, and bits of commentary. All of these function differently from topical material. Topical material conveys information about actions, events, and states of affairs in the world. Metadiscourse helps readers organize, classify, interpret, evaluate, and react to such information. It can be added to virtually any topical material.

Exercise Three

Identify the elements in each of the following sentences that are examples of metadiscourse, and name the kind of metadiscourse each one is. For example, in *Alarmingly, it is certain that he fell from the cliff*, there are two kinds of metadiscourse. *Alarmingly* is an attitude marker, and *it is certain that* is a modality marker.

1. It is undoubtedly the case that a disciplinary approach to education will become more popular.
2. What we will discover in the last chapter is that all of his efforts are misguided.
3. Fortunately, Tom brought some wisdom to the discussion of Victorian sensibilities.
4. You will probably not welcome being told that this system of logic is seriously flawed.
5. At the same time, the company decided to change its marketing strategy.
6. I conclude by noting that only a few of you will have the courage to resist materialism.
7. It seems that those multi-national corporations are becoming increasingly powerful.
8. The provost reported that the college had won an award for recruiting minority faculty members.

9. It is most satisfying to report that three of our seniors have won prestigious national fellowships.

10. In the second place, however, his view on aesthetics denies the role of cultural change.

Exercise Four

One of the best ways to learn about the kinds and functions of metadiscourse is to write some of it. In each of the following cases, write a sentence that includes the kind or kinds of metadiscourse specified. For example, if you were asked to write a sentence with a connective indicating a relationship of logic, you could write *Therefore, the claim was dismissed.*

1. A connective indicating a relationship of time.
2. A connective indicating a relationship of logic.
3. A connective reminding readers of topical material presented earlier.
4. An action marker.
5. A modality marker that hedges.
6. A modality marker that stresses that some topical material is true.
7. A modality marker that indicates in which personal framework something is true.
8. A narrator.
9. An attitude marker.
10. Some commentary on how readers should read a section of an essay.

METADISCOURSE AND
SENTENCE PATTERNS

Metadiscourse can be all that appears in some sentences. Consider this one:

> Having made this point, I wish to add a necessary qualification.
>
> (Robert Scholes, *Textual Power*, p. 144)

This sentence moves from a connective into an action marker, one that performs an action related to marking modality.

But I have spent some time on metadiscourse here primarily because when it is added to strings of topical material, it usually produces a pattern-three or pattern-five sentence. Not all kinds of metadiscourse work this way, but many do.

For example, if we add certain kinds of metadiscourse to the beginning of a string of topical material, we will usually get a pattern-three sentence. Consider the topical string *aerobic dance keeps one fit.* If we add an action marker to it (*I conclude by noting that*), we get a pattern-three sentence:

FE, S   T

   I conclude by noting that aerobic dance keeps one fit.

Likewise, if we add a modality marker (*I firmly believe that*) to the topical string, we get a pattern-three sentence:

FE, S   T

   I firmly believe that aerobic dance keeps one fit.

The same is true if we add a narrator (*Mrs. Schmerz reports that*), an attitude marker (*I am amazed that*), or some commentary (*You will be happy to hear that*).

If we add two kinds of metadiscourse to the beginning of a topical string, we usually get a pattern-five sentence. We have to be careful about combining kinds of metadiscourse, and about their order. But pattern-five sentences are usually the results.

For instance, if we add an action marker (*In conclusion*) and a modality marker (*I think it is possible that*), we get a pattern-five sentence:

FE   S   T

In conclusion, I think it is possible that aerobic dance keeps one fit.

The same is true if we add a connective (*In the third place*) and a narrator (*Mr. Beiner says that*):

FE   S   T

In the third place, Mr. Beiner says that aerobic dance keeps one fit.

I focus on pattern-three and pattern-five sentences because, of the five patterns, they are the main ones working against the second guideline. In other words, if you want to make your sentence topics clearly identifiable for readers, you will generally avoid writing sentences following patterns three and five.

Several research studies have examined effective and ineffective essays written on the same subject matter. When researchers examined the kinds of sentences in both sets, they found that neither set contained many pattern-four sentences. More important, they found that the effective essays had a high proportion of pattern-one and pattern-two sentences, and that the ineffective essays had a high proportion of pattern-three and pattern-five sentences.

Therefore, there is probably a connection between kinds of sentences and raters' perceptions of overall quality. And I would say that there is a connection between the ease with which readers can identify sentence topics and their judgments of high quality in essays. For in pattern-three and pattern-five sentences, the topic appears neither early nor in the main subject, places where readers look first to find it. In such sentences, therefore, readers have to search longer to find the topic. And that search probably leads them to see the essay as somewhat unclear or frustrating.

In this light, we can better understand why so many composition textbooks warn against sentences beginning with the expletives *there* (*There are things that I should say to you*) or *it* (*It is my considered opinion that spring vacation should be extended*). These textbooks note that *there* and *it* are usually followed by some form of *to be* and then a noun. And they point out that such a sequence produces very little movement or action in a sentence and thus should be avoided.

In the main I agree. But an additional factor here is that the *there* and *it* usually appear where readers expect to find sentence topics. Instead of topics, they find empty words.

We can also better understand why so many teachers and textbooks warn against "writing about your own writing," which is essentially what you do with metadiscourse. The typical justification for this warning is that "writing about your own writing" is always useless padding. No one should underestimate how powerful the attraction of such padding can be. One of my students told me that she frequently confronts assignments for which she needs eight pages but can come up with only four. What does she do? She uses, she says, "whatever takes up more space," which includes generous helpings of metadiscourse.

Again, in the main I agree with warnings against "writing about your own writing." But I add that a more nearly complete justification for them would include the idea that the metadiscourse often appears precisely where readers expect to find topics. Finding none there, they must try to remember the nature of the metadiscourse while they search further for topics. And that can be difficult and tiring. Moreover, metadiscourse can be misleading, even for writers. When weaker writers start sentences with bits of metadiscourse such as *I think that* or *I am amazed that*, they run some serious risks. They can lose the way and go on to develop paragraphs as if they were about themselves and not about the original subject matter.

This point is always reinforced for me when I ask students what they think the sentence *I hypothesize that nuclear war is a great threat to civilization* is essentially about. Some say it is about the person that *I* refers to. These students have lost their way after only one sentence, since the topic of the sentence is, of course, *nuclear war*.

To sum up at this point, I would say that we make our topics most clearly identifiable for our readers if we express them early or as the subjects of sentences. Generally, we should write more pattern-one and pattern-two sentences. At the same time, we should write fewer pattern-three and pattern-five sentences. Pattern-four sentences, although they express the topic early, usually seem fairly complex and wordy and probably should be used sparingly.

Simply writing more pattern-one and pattern-two sentences, however, will not ensure that readers will identify all of our topics easily. As we will see in greater detail in Chapter Six, we can also get into trouble by packing too much information into topics. Sometimes we do this by using long noun clauses or noun phrases.

Consider the following sentence:

> Positive reinforcement by supervisory personnel and others of the responses by disadvantaged learners that lead to their successful integration into regular classrooms must be encouraged.

One of the problems with this sentence is that its topic includes more than we can take in without strain. We have to work to figure out what this sentence is about. In fact, in such sentences, much of the actual message is probably spread throughout the topic and not the comment, where it belongs. Such a sentence would function better with a shorter topic and a longer comment:

> Supervisory personnel and others should react positively to the responses of disadvantaged learners that lead to their successful integration into regular classrooms.

This sentence could be made clearer still, but note for now that changing the topic makes a great difference, even without making further improvements.

JUSTIFIED METADISCOURSE?

Does my warning about pattern-three and pattern-five sentences mean that we should never use expletives or some kinds of metadiscourse? No.

Often an initial *there* functions well. Many skilled writers use it as a topicalizer, often to introduce topics that will be commented on in several sentences in a row. Lewis Thomas does this in the following sentence, in which he topicalizes everything after *There is*, making the sentence practically all topic:

> There is ambiguity, and some symbolism, in the elaborate ritual observed by each returning expedition of astronauts from the moon.
>
> ("Thoughts for a Countdown," *The Lives of a Cell*, p. 5)

He then goes on to devote extensive commentary to the ambiguity and symbolism.

In addition, many skilled writers use a *there is* or *there are* construction to add a more general and less personal emphasis to points. For example, writers could produce *I find much to admire in Kant's style*. But if they want to make the judgment seem less dependent on them and more generally justified, they would probably choose to write *There is much to admire in Kant's style*.

Finally, we are almost forced to use a *there is* or *there are* when the only alternative would be to write that something exists when it is not customary to describe that something as existing. For example, I would not wish to change *There is a vision in the land* to *A vision exists in the land* because we do not typically speak of visions as existing. Nor would I wish to change the sentence *There is a dearth of material on that subject*. To say that *a dearth exists* would be unusual and would strain the bounds of logic.

What about metadiscourse generally? Should we avoid it? One way to move toward an answer is to see whether established writers use it. And many do, often substantial amounts of it.

Almost every printed page will contain some kind of connective. I open Carl Sagan's *The Dragons of Eden* at random and find:

> On the contrary, the model may help us to understand what human beings are about. (p. 64)

At one point John Updike uses the following very striking action marker:

But let it be admitted—nay, proclaimed—that by and large Mr. McGahern writes entrancingly, with a lively pace and constant melody.

("An Old-Fashioned Novel," *Hugging the Shore*, p. 390)

George L. Dillon uses a modality marker in the following:

Perceptual strategies, we have postulated, are useful for making quick decisions on limited information.

(*Language Processing and the Reading of Literature*, p. 22)

William H. Gass uses the following narrator:

As Kafka says, the writer does not copy the world, or explain it, but declares his dissatisfaction with it, and suffers.

("The Soul Inside the Sentence," *Habitations of the Word*, p. 137)

Carl Sagan writes the following attitude marker:

Fortunately, the relevant physics is extremely simple and can be performed to order of magnitude even without any consideration of gravitation.

(*Broca's Brain*, p. 116)

And early in an essay Susumu Kuno offers some commentary to his readers:

Those readers who have little interest in Japanese may proceed immediately to § 6, where the examination of English counterparts of the *wa* and *ga* distinction starts.

("Functional Sentence Perspective: A Case Study from Japanese and English, *Linguistic Inquiry, 3*, p. 270)

Finally, writers frequently string together several kinds of metadiscourse at the beginning of a sentence.

Peter Trudgill uses an action marker and a connective to introduce a sentence about a list of differences among social-class dialects:

It must be emphasized, too, that this list does not supply any hard and fast rules for usage by different groups. . . .

(*Sociolinguistics: An Introduction*, p. 62)

Geoffrey Sampson uses a connective and a modality marker:

However, it is surely quite wrong to assume, because the *Sprachgeist* notion is admittedly nonsensical, that Schleicher's equation of linguistics with biology must necessarily be given up too.

(*Schools of Linguistics*, p. 28)

And John Lyons uses an attitude marker (that shades into an action marker), a connective, and a modality marker to introduce a sentence about transformational grammar:

> It is important to realize, however, that, as far as Chomsky is concerned, the notion of deep structure still plays much the same role in syntax as it always has done in his formalization of transformational grammar.
>
> (*Noam Chomsky* (revised edition), p. 98)

In the light of such citations, it would be foolish for me to proclaim a hard and fast rule against metadiscourse and against pattern-three and pattern-five sentences. But I would still urge you to identify all such sentences in your early drafts and then see if you can justify them. If you cannot, you should revise them.

But you will be able to make a good case for some of them. Narrators you should retain, unless, of course, they are unnecessary because of what you are sure your readers know. Many of the other kinds of metadiscourse will depend for their justification on aspects of your writing situation. For example, with readers who will probably need a good deal of help with your presentation, you might decide to justify more than a minimal number of connectives, action markers, and bits of commentary. You might have to help them more as they move through your presentation. This is probably why many writing teachers call for the frequent use of connectives.

Similarly, in a context in which revealing your personality might not be out of place or might even be expected, you might choose to include some attitude markers or bits of commentary.

And when you are unsure of the status of the information you convey (Is it fact? opinion? mere conjecture?), you would be wise to hedge it. Too many of my students present opinions and hypotheses as if they were facts. Apparently they think that the more forcefully they make a claim, the more likely their readers are to accept it. But if readers know the claim is not factual, they may come to distrust everything the students write.

In summary, it all depends—on who your readers are, on what you think they know, on what your purpose for writing is, on what level of formality an essay seeking to achieve such a purpose should probably have, and on what the status of your information is. You should read many other writers, analyze the contexts of their writing, see how they use metadiscourse, and then judge how effectively they use it. And try to hear how their and your specimens of prose sound. Often reading prose aloud can help you decide whether a writer has done too much "writing about writing." You will become sensitive to the writer's voice affecting the topical material. For example, one of my students recently used reading aloud to discover how tentative he sounded at the end of a persuasive paper, where he should have been assertive but where he began four of five sentences with the modality marker *It seems.*

Then turn back to your own drafts and have a reason for the pattern-three sentences and pattern-five sentences that you use. My guess is that usually you will not be able to justify a large number of such sentences. But those you do justify can help you meet your readers' minds and achieve your purposes in writing.

Exercise Five

Revise each of the following sentences by cutting out all metadiscourse. And if you thereby change the meaning, be prepared to describe the change. For example, from the sentence *I hypothesize that the universe holds other intelligent beings*, you should cut out *I hypothesize that.* Doing so does change the meaning, turning a hypothesis into an apparent statement of fact.

1. I begin by noting that the writing-across-the-curriculum proposal has been before you for two months.
2. Fortunately, she had finished her work on the word processor when the electricity was turned off.
3. I believe that Carol drove a new Corvette to campus today.
4. In the second place, therefore, democracy must take slightly different forms in different cultures.
5. Some readers may find it surprising to learn that the analytic theory is correct.
6. At the same time, I should add that, in Wittgenstein's view, only propositions have sense.
7. Therefore, it is the committee's belief that all freshmen should learn how to compose their essays on a word processor.
8. We conclude this chapter by adding that, in our opinion, Aristotle's approach to art as imitation is without equal.

9. Nonetheless, it is most assuredly the case that the wrestling metaphor is inappropriate for his purpose.
10. Unfortunately, however, they missed the ferry by a minute.

Exercise Six

Some of the following sentences contain modality markers and some do not. Tell which of those with modality markers should keep them and which would be better without them. Also, tell which of those sentences without modality markers should remain without them and which should have modality markers added to them. In all cases, be prepared to justify your answer.

For example, *The universe holds other intelligent beings* has no modality marker in it. It should have a hedge, however (something like *They think that* or *perhaps*), since this sentence, to the best of our knowledge, does not express a fact.

1. In my opinion, no women can read a map well.
2. Men are crass and insensitive.
3. Many scientists hypothesize that all the elemental forces of nature are elegantly interrelated.
4. Pro-life advocates contend that abortion is the murder of a human being.
5. In large American cities, racial integration will never succeed.
6. It is our opinion that the moon also exerts some gravitational pull on the earth.
7. Evolution operates in an orderly and predictable fashion.
8. I have always suspected that Marlowe wrote many of Shakespeare's plays.
9. Those theologians proclaimed that "God is dead!"
10. The problems that Canada has had with acid rain are entirely the fault of the United States, and therefore the United States should pay for the damage to Canadian resources.

TO REVIEW:
EXPRESSING SENTENCE TOPICS

Earlier chapters have shown the importance of topics. This chapter stresses expressing topics so that readers can find them easily and efficiently. The primary impediments to readers' finding your topics easily are sentence patterns in which the first element and the subject are the same, but both of these are different from the topic, and in which the first element, the subject, and the topic are all different. Most often, such kinds of sentences result when writers use types of metadiscourse to introduce their sentences. Therefore, metadiscourse should be scrutinized carefully and justified as a part of your essays. In many cases, much of it should be edited out. But some of it can help you achieve your purposes in writing.

FURTHER READING

Crismore, A. (1984). "The Rhetoric of Textbooks: Metadiscourse," *Journal of Curriculum Studies, 16,* 279-296.

Lautamatti, L. (1980). "Subject and Theme in English Discourse." In K. Sajavaara and J. Lehtonen (Eds.), *Papers in Discourse and Contrastive Discourse Analysis* (pp. 188-201). Jyväskylä: University of Jyväskylä.

Vande Kopple, W. J. (1985). "Some Exploratory Discourse on Metadiscourse," *College Composition and Communication, 36,* 82-93.

Williams, J. M. (1985). "The Grammar of Concision," *Style: Ten Lessons in Clarity and Grace* (2nd ed.). Glenview, IL: Scott, Foresman.

Witte, S. P. (1983). "Topical Structure and Writing Quality: Some Possible Text-Based Explanations of Readers' Judgments of Student Writing," *Visible Language, 17,* 177-205.

CHAPTER

Crafting Sentence Comments

The linear geometry of the sentence imposes certain relationships upon the elements that compose it.
—Dwight Bolinger, "Linear Modification"

"Would you tell me, please, which way I ought to go from here?" "That depends a good deal on where you want to get to," said the Cat.
—Lewis Carroll, *Alice's Adventures in Wonderland*

The end of a matter is better than its beginning. . . .
—Ecclesiastes 7:8 (NIV)

U p to this point, I have focused on guidelines for sentence topics. Now I would like to focus on a guideline for comments. Comments, you recall, usually correspond to the grammatical predicate of a sentence. More roughly, we can say that the comment includes everything after the topic.

THE THIRD GUIDELINE

The third guideline is as follows: In general, use sentence comments to express the central message about your topics, and, whenever possible, use the very end of the comment to express the most important part of that message.

In each sentence, readers pay special attention to two points -the beginning and the end. As we saw earlier, the beginning usually includes the topic. The beginning is where readers look to get their bearings, to find out what a sentence is about. The end of a sentence is usually part of its comment. The end is where readers look to find the most important information in a sentence, the information that is the point of the sentence.

None of this material is meant to suggest that the middle of a sentence is insignificant. But I do mean to suggest that writers must perform at least two different acts with their sentences: They must hold up the subjects of their messages (in topics) for their readers to see, and they must convey information about those subjects (in comments).

If writers were to hold up topics without conveying information about them, most readers would find the message boring or frustrating. A few more inventive and long-suffering readers might see the topics as clues in a kind of guessing game. But, after a while, such a game would lose its appeal. On the other hand, if writers were to convey information without indicating what it is about, readers would find the message mysterious and confusing. When we write, therefore, we contract with our readers to perform both of these acts appropriately.

To make these claims more specific and plausible, consider some evidence that the end of a string of words expresses what is the point or very nearly the point of that string. The end qualifies everything that comes before it.

This is true even for many short phrases. Contrast *at the appointed hour* with *at the hour appointed*. In the first, *hour* carries the essential information. We actually accept *appointed* without question and start to consider the significance of the hour as a unit of time (as opposed to, say, a minute or a day). We start to wonder, "When is this hour? What's so special about it?"

In *at the hour appointed*, however, we do not wonder what is special about the hour (as opposed to a minute or a day). Here *appointed* carries the essential information. We start to think about the act of appointing ("Who appointed it? Why?").

My point is probably clearer when applied to clauses. Contrast

> Why did you quickly withdraw the motion?

with

> Why did you withdraw the motion quickly?

The first sentence ends with *withdraw the motion*, thereby expressing a concern about why the motion was withdrawn. Its writer is basically asking, "Why did you withdraw the motion at all?" On the other hand, the peak of information in the second sentence appears in *quickly*. Here the basic concern is with speed. The writer of this sentence is essentially saying, "I know you withdrew the motion, but why did you do it quickly?"

Similarly, contrast

> In order to prepare for class, he had to hide out in the library

with

> He had to hide out in the library in order to prepare for class.

The first sentence makes a point essentially about where he went. The second sentence makes a point about his reasons for hiding out in the library.

The principle that I am illustrating also holds for many sentences with more than one clause. Contrast

> I'll grade your term papers as soon as you hand them in

with

> As soon as you hand them in, I'll grade your term papers.

Here the first sentence makes a point essentially about when the grading will occur. The second makes a point about what will happen when the papers come in.

It is true that these phrases and sentences appear here out of context. It is also true that not all sentences in English allow us to revise their comments radically. But the phrases and sentences that appear here illustrate quite well the principle underlying the third guideline: The end of a sentence should convey the most important information in the sentence; it should provide the primary response to the concern that motivated the sentence in the first place.

Thus, even at the level of the individual sentence, we see that style depends on the writing situation because the proper form of sentences depends to a great extent on what writers think their readers' concerns and expectations are. Of course, writers can do much with their sentence topics to create and channel those concerns. But once they create such concerns, they should respond to them primarily at the end of their comments.

The best writers do this well; perhaps they get things right in every sentence the first time. Most of us, though, need to review and revise our sentences to make sure we do not violate the third guideline without good reason.

Exercise One

Tell what the essential point or message of each of the following sentences is. Then tell what question or concern each of these probably responds to. For example, the essential point of *They sent the keys yesterday* has to do with time. It responds to a question or concern about when they sent the keys.

1a. They were running in the rain.
1b. In the rain they were running.
2a. You should go to Denmark in the spring.
2b. In the spring you should go to Denmark.

3a. Why did you angrily leave the gymnasium?
3b. Why did you leave the gymnasium angrily?
4a. She applied for a leave of absence, since she wanted to finish her novel.
4b. Since she wanted to finish her novel, she applied for a leave of absence.
5a. We will vote on this motion when the secretary gets here.
5b. When the secretary gets here, we will vote on this motion.

MATERIAL THAT USUALLY SHOULD NOT APPEAR AT THE END OF COMMENTS

Metadiscourse

Many writers express material at the end of their comments that they should not, since it is not the most important information in sentences. For example, some writers end sentences with kinds of metadiscourse. As we noted earlier, of course, they should first of all justify the metadiscourse. But even if they can, they should normally not express it at the end of sentences, for this material by its very nature does not convey information about topics. It helps readers organize, evaluate, and react to such information. It is difficult to imagine, therefore, that it could provide the main point for very many sentences.

The kinds of metadiscourse that I most often see at the end of sentences are connectives, action markers, modality markers, and narrators. I find sentences such as the following:

> Those who establish rewards for good teaching must examine all the implications of their decisions, however.
>
> Teachers of composition should spend more time in conferences with students, for example.
>
> College education in the United States should never have lost its liberal arts foundation, I believe.

And here are two sentences from a student's paper I received recently, the second sentence of which ends with a narrator:

> In 1967 Eric Lenneberg "proposed a critical period for the development of human language," suggesting that language is a "function of brain maturation and develops 'from mere exposure' to a linguistic environment only during a critical period" (1977, p. 207). This period

ranges from about the age of two years to puberty, according to Lenneberg.

Elements such as *however, for example, I believe*, and *according to Lenneberg* may be close to the point of some sentences. Occasionally you will find such elements last in sentences composed by skilled writers. For instance, in a review of a novel by Günter Grass, John Updike complains that in the novel it is difficult to find a central thread. He describes how Grass goes on at length about several apparently unrelated subjects. Grass seems to preach at length about whatever comes to his mind. Then Updike uses the following short sentence: "He [Grass] spouts off, in short" ("The Squeeze Is On," *Hugging the Shore*, p. 485).

Here Updike does exactly what I have just warned against. He leaves some metadiscourse (*in short*, which functions primarily as a connective but also, probably, as an action marker) at the end. Is this a mistake? Should Updike have written, "In short, he spouts off"? Perhaps you would say that this sentence is so short that it makes little difference where *in short* appears. But I think that Updike knew exactly what he was doing. By placing *in short* at the end, he draws special attention to it. And as a message it stands in direct and striking contrast to what Updike has just claimed Grass does: carrying on at length about several subjects without sufficient control over them.

Usually, however, elements of metadiscourse are not the most important in a sentence. At the end of a sentence, they may even strike readers as letdowns.

My advice, therefore, is first to justify using elements of metadiscourse and then to decide whether they are close to the point of your sentence. If they are not, you should express them early in your sentence, most likely at the beginning.

This will leave you with sentences such as these:

> However, those who establish rewards for good teaching must examine all the implications of their decisions.

> For example, teachers of composition should spend more time in conferences with their students.

Such a transformation moves information that is not the most important in each sentence away from the end. And it lets readers know from the start how they are to view and process the material that follows. This can be an important aid to readers.

Imagine reading a long sentence and then finding a *however* at the end. Unless there are obvious clues in the nature of the material about how to read the sentence, you would read it the first time without knowing that all the information is intended to make a contrasting or opposing point. So once you discover the *however*, you may actually have to review some of the information that precedes it to make sure you have interpreted the sentence correctly.

Similarly, imagine reading a sentence that you take to be factual, only to discover an *according to our preliminary hypothesis* at the end. Suddenly you would have to change your view of the information in that sentence. And perhaps you would want to review that information to judge its validity for yourself. Such stopping, starting, and going back over what you have read can be irritating and confusing. Giving readers signals such as *however* and *according to our preliminary hypothesis* first in a sentence probably saves them time and keeps them from irritation and confusion.

Some skilled writers object to placing elements such as *however* first in a sentence. They say that doing so makes a style heavy and reveals a writer too obviously concerned with giving readers signals. In this claim there is something worth considering. But if you read respected writers with a critical eye on their style, you will notice that many of them begin sentences with words such as *however*. The key issue is to what degree you want to associate such elements with the focal point of sentences. First position associates them with the focal point more strongly than middle positions do, thereby giving them more emphasis. You would opt for first position, therefore, when you really need to stress the signal conveyed by such words. For example, you might choose to express a *however* first when the contrasting point it signals is very important or will probably surprise readers.

But even when you do not need that much emphasis, I would still say that you should usually place such elements early in sentences. You could settle on forms such as the following:

> College education in the United States, I believe, should never have lost its liberal arts foundation.

> The second reason for applying to your law school is that, as your informative brochure points out, your program has a strong service orientation.

Such sentences still have the metadiscourse fairly early, and at the end they have the information that deserves to be stressed.

Orienters

Other kinds of elements usually should not appear last in a sentence. These elements set the stage for the sentence, showing where or when the action or event described takes place. Such orienting information usually is not the most important in a sentence.

One of my students used the following sentence in a paper about creative ways to foster language development:

> Y. P. Catching found some evidence that art enhances reading skills in his 1984 study.

Here the phrase "in his 1984 study" orients readers to which of Catching's studies the writer is concerned with. It is not the most important information in this sentence; the information about art enhancing reading skills is. Moreover, as it stands, this sentence could strike readers as ambiguous, if only for a moment: Did Catching find in his 1984 study that art enhances students' reading skills, or did art enhance the reading skills in or of the 1984 study? Thus, this sentence should be revised so that the phrase appears earlier, perhaps at the beginning.

Another of my students, while working on an essay about his brothers, described the crazy things they had done. At one point he used the following sentence:

> They fed donkeys Bit O' Honey candy, which practically glued their teeth together during a trip to the Grand Canyon.

I viewed the phrase *during a trip to the Grand Canyon* as not among the most important elements in the sentence. Also, as it stands here, it may make readers imagine that the donkeys took the trip to the Grand Canyon with the boys. Thus I asked my student whether it really should appear last. After some thought, he moved the phrase into first position, where it sets the stage for the rest of the material. In addition, when the phrase is moved, the sentence can end with the humorous details about the donkeys with their teeth nearly stuck together.

Recoverable Material

Still other kinds of material that ordinarily should not appear last in a sentence are bits of information that have been included before that sentence or that could be inferred from material preceding that sentence. Such bits of information, since they are recoverable from earlier material and to a great extent point backwards, usually will not be the most important bits in a sentence.

All of the following sentences end weakly with information that is recoverable from sentences that would precede them:

> Professor Olson is one such person.
>
> The pathways in the grass on the quadrangles are still another result of their lack of respect for the beauty of the campus.
>
> Compassion is her most striking trait.
>
> The gift of the forest preserve is the third example of their generosity to the college.

The elements in these sentences could be moved around so that the information that readers are less familiar with could come last. The first sentence, for example, could be revised as follows:

> One such person is Professor Olson.

The words *such person* clearly connect to material that would appear before this sentence.

We have to be particularly on guard to make such switches in writing, since we often do not make them in speech. When I was young, I traveled with my family to Ontario. At the border, a customs officer, hearing that we were from Grand Rapids, asked what we made in Grand Rapids. I knew an answer, and I blurted it out: "We make furniture in Grand Rapids." If I had had a chance to revise that sentence, of course, I would have put *In Grand Rapids* (which was already in the air) first, and *furniture* (which was the point of the answer) last.

Similarly, a few weeks before I wrote this sentence, one of my colleagues said the following in our conference room:

> A good deal of care about salt intake is essential. You'll get high blood pressure if you use too much salt.

If he had the chance to recast the second sentence, he would be wise to reverse the order of the two clauses. He should position *If you use too much salt* (which is closely related to the sentence before it) first, and *you'll get high blood pressure* (which is the point of the second sentence) last.

POSITIONING FREE MODIFIERS IN SENTENCES

Sometimes, though, it is difficult to decide whether a particular bit of information should be expressed at the very end of a sentence, or at least in the comment. It is often difficult to decide what to do with modifiers that could appear in several different positions.

I have judged several fine arts contests for students in junior and senior high schools, and in their writing I often find sentences such as these:

> A tall and proud heron stood in the shallows.
>
> The rolling, curling, billowing clouds marched across the sky.

The modifiers here are clichés or close to clichés, of course, and maybe they do not work well together. But neither of these concerns is my main one here. My concern is that they appear in the topics of the sentences. There they will not receive the kind of attention they deserve if they are supposed to be part of the essential message of each sentence. In a sense, expressing such modifiers in a topic (which readers tend to accept without debate or challenge) robs them of their informing power or punch.

Now perhaps these modifiers are not supposed to be among the most important elements in their sentences. When I look at the comments of these sentences, though, I am led to believe that the writers intended the modifiers to be part of their core message. But they apparently do not know how to position them to accomplish that or did not think about accomplishing that.

How would a more skilled writer position such modifiers if he or she wanted readers to see them as the most important elements in the sentences? Probably in a manner close to the following:

> A heron stood in the shallows; it was tall and proud.

or

> A heron stood in the shallows, tall and proud.
>
> The clouds marched across the sky; they were rolling, curling, and billowing.

or

> The clouds marched across the sky, rolling, curling, billowing.

Trying to decide what your most important information in each sentence is can be tedious and counterproductive as you compose early drafts of essays. At that stage you should be concerned primarily with discovering and organizing useful material. So wait to make decisions about the importance of information until you revise and edit. If information is close to the point of a sentence, try to express it in the sentence comment. If it is the point of the sentence, try to position it at the very end of the comment.

Exercise Two

Some of the following sentences clearly have weak comments. Identify them and revise them so that they end with what seems to be the core of their message. For example, the sentence *The primary election will be closely contested, I think* ends weakly with some metadiscourse. It should be revised to read *I think that the primary election will be closely contested* or *The primary election, I think, will be closely contested*. Or you might argue for deleting the metadiscourse altogether.

1. The student's appeal should never have been brought to that committee, nevertheless.
2. Ernie caught the two salmon using a lure called a western wobbly.
3. Trying to decide what information to express in sentence comments is best accomplished during later stages of the writing process, in conclusion.
4. Janel is another teacher who takes undergraduate education seriously.
5. The course in the philosophy of law should be at the center of that program, I have always believed.
6. Lately, his prose has been dull, self-conscious, and predictable.
7. I am applying to Almater College because it is a college for those who wish to learn how to improve society, according to the very attractive college catalog.
8. Graciousness is an even more noticeable part of her personality.
9. We shall have to poll the faculty to determine what they think of students' writing abilities, in the second place.
10. Since receiving his degree, he has specialized in modern literature and criticism.

Exercise Three

Below are sentences you should try to imitate. Retain their basic structure and the logical connections among the material expressed in the various parts of the structure while using material that you invent. For example, if you were asked to imitate *A second necessary feature of good student teachers is confidence*, you might choose to write something like *A third essential ingredient for spicy Dutch apple pie is cinnamon*.

1. Her report on careers outside of teaching was clear, succinct, and persuasive.
2. A third reason to support the amendment is that it should encourage more student involvement in the governance of the college.
3. Another person who influenced them positively was Professor Schlussel.
4. In our opinion, the university has not made a sufficiently strong commitment to its undergraduates.
5. His letter of application was perfect in form but flat in tone.
6. The bird was playing under the waterfall, dipping, bobbing, and splashing.
7. Even more surprising than their idealism was their resilience in the classroom.
8. I shall begin by pointing out that the problem of reverse discrimination is an old one.
9. Finally, still another cause for some concern is the declining level of alumni contributions to the general fund.
10. His short story is moving without being sentimental, directive without being didactic.

SYNTACTIC STRUCTURES THAT HIGHLIGHT COMMENTS

So far we have examined two techniques that we can use to conclude our sentences with their most important information. We can move less important information away from the end, often to the beginning:

He proceeded to define the essence of literary texts, in the second place can be changed to

> In the second place, he proceeded to define the essence of literary texts.

Or in sentences with certain verbs, we can get less important information out of comments by reversing subjects and complements:

> Professor Canton is another teacher who taught us important things about writing

can be reversed to

> Another teacher who taught us important things about writing was Professor Canton.

Before concluding this chapter, I wish to describe some syntactic structures that we can use not to move information out of comments but to call extra attention to the information that deserves to be in them. You recall that final position in a sentence in itself calls attention to information. Since the three structures that I will describe call even more attention to information, they are normally used only when circumstances warrant heavy attention on comments.

The *What*-Cleft

The word *cleft* is a part of this name because when we produce one of these, we first must cleave a sentence in two, right after the main verb. Then we add a *what* to the beginning of the sentence and the appropriate form of *to be* after the original verb. Thus, each part of the cleft ends up with its own verb. For example, we can start with

> They bought a house in Lowell.

We cleave it after the verb:

> They bought   a house in Lowell.

Then we make the necessary additions:

> What they bought was a house in Lowell.

In these forms, the elements through the form of *to be* convey information already known to readers. In our example, the writer assumes that readers know that those referred to by the *they* have already bought something. All elements after the form of *to be* (the comment) are treated as elements that readers do not already know about. The *what*-cleft focuses special attention on that which readers need to learn.

As with the syntactic devices that topicalize elements of a sentence, the *what*-cleft has special functions.

The first part of it often functions as a kind of metadiscourse. Someone could write *I think that* but chooses instead to write *What I think is that*. The same is true of combinations such as *I argue that* (*What I argue is that*), *I conclude that* (*What I conclude is that*), and *The dean announced that* (*What the dean announced was that*).

When would the early portion of *what*-clefts function as metadiscourse? Often these clefts appear at important junctures in essays. They can signal proposals, turns in the argument, the examining of an opponent's claims, and conclusions. For example, here is James Boyd White alerting readers to his agenda:

> What I hope to show is how these conceptions [of the equal value of other people, of integrating parts of oneself] arise from a reading of these texts and are given by them a vastly richer and more biting content than any summary statement can possibly have.
>
> (*When Words Lose Their Meanings*, p. 18)

But there is more to it. Skilled writers generally do not use forms such as *What I believe is that* unless they wish to give a strong clarification of an issue or a forceful reply to a question that they can reasonably predict their readers would be asking. They write *What I believe is that* when they imagine their readers saying, "We've heard all sorts of hypotheses. Now tell us where you take your stance." When teaching, I rarely say *What I mean is that* unless the looks on my students' faces show me that they have little idea what I mean or when they tell me that I have been unclear. Similarly, the following *what*-cleft shows Stanley Fish working to clarify what he thinks his readers might be wondering about:

> What I am suggesting is that there is no direct relationship between the meaning of a sentence (paragraph, novel, poem) and what its words mean.
>
> ("Literature in the Reader: Affective Stylistics,"
> in *Reader-Response Criticism*, p. 77)

Often *what*-clefts respond to readers' probable questions or concerns by showing contrasts. Their function is to invest the point of contrasts with a great deal of force. We hear them used this way in speech rather often. In one episode of *Miami Vice*, for example, a powerful banker asks Detective Crockett something like, "You sure you wouldn't want a drink?" Crockett responds emphatically with a *what*-cleft: "What I want is answers!"

In writing, many *what*-clefts function similarly. S. Michael Halloran provides a good example of this:

> What they [Watson and Crick] offer is not *the* structure of DNA or *a* model of DNA, but Watson and Crick's structure or model.
>
> ("The Birth of Molecular Biology: An Essay in the Rhetorical Criticism of Scientific Discourse," *Rhetoric Review*, 3, 1984, 75)

The *It*-Cleft (1)

Another pattern that highlights comments also is formed by cleaving a sentence in two. Usually we cut between the subject and the predicate. Then we add an *It is* or *It was* before the subject and a *who*, *that*, or *which* before the predicate. To illustrate, we can start with

Clare studied literary criticism.

We cleave the sentence:

Clare   studied literary criticism.

And then we add the appropriate elements:

It was Clare who studied literary criticism.

Or we can do the same with the form that fronts *literary criticism*:

It was literary criticism that Clare studied.

Sometimes we cleave a sentence after an introductory phrase. Then we add an *It is* or *It was* before the phrase and a *who*, *that*, or *which* after it. For example, we start with

In 1968 he went to West Germany.

We cleave the sentence:

In 1968   he went to West Germany.

And then we add the appropriate elements:

> It was in 1968 that he went to West Germany.

As we will see, there are at least two kinds of *it*-clefts, each with its own functions. What happens in the first kind is that writers mention something in one sentence and then later refer to it in the topic of an *it*-cleft right after the *it is* or *it was*. They go on to add a significant comment about the topic, a comment whose significance they often signal with the word *indeed*.

For example, one of my students uses such an *it*-cleft in an essay on the total physical response method of teaching foreign languages:

> In the back of the room, the home base chairs should be positioned. It is in these chairs that the students perform the actions to the commands of the teacher for all the others to see.

This comment is significant because performing actions in response to commands is at the center of this method.

Similarly, E. B. White describes a dragonfly alighting on the tip of his fishing rod as he fishes with his son. The dragonfly reminds White of one that had rested on the tip of his rod when as a boy he had fished with his father. He then writes the following *it*-cleft:

> It was the arrival of this fly that convinced me beyond any doubt that everything was as it always had been, that the years were a mirage and that there had been no years.
>
> ("Once More to the Lake")

White uses the *it*-cleft to topicalize the arrival of the fly and then to add to it a comment that is close to the heart of his essay.

The first kind of *it*-cleft can also signal contrasts, sometimes implicitly. It is as if writers say to us, "This particular topic and only this topic can be attached to this important comment." Thus we often find words such as *this very* or *precisely this* before the topic. For example, consider one of Wolfgang Iser's sentences as he argues that readers' understandings of a literary work cannot be completely controlled by that work:

> . . . and, indeed, it is the very lack of control that forms the basis of the creative side of reading.
>
> (*The Act of Reading*, p. 108.)

The *It*-Cleft (2)

In the second kind of *it*-cleft, the nature of the information in each section of the sentence is different from what it is in the first kind. In the first, the information that appears after the *It is* or *It was* is familiar to readers. In fact, that information probably appeared only a sentence or two before the *it*-cleft. And the information that appears after the *It was x that* is treated as probably not previously known by readers.

In the second kind of *it*-cleft, the information that follows the *It was* or *It is* is not available to readers from earlier sentences or the situation. But the information that follows the *It was x that* is treated as recoverable.

For example, in a sentence such as *It was spring break that gave them a chance to visit Leland*, *spring break* is treated as unfamiliar to readers and *that gave them a chance to visit Leland* is treated as something that readers already know.

What I am going to say now will surprise you at first, since it seems to contradict much of what I have stressed so far. In the second kind of *it*-cleft, the comment precedes the topic. That is, *spring break* is the comment in the sample sentence, and a time *that gave them a chance to visit Leland* is the topic. Naming spring break is the purpose of this sentence. This sentence responds to the question "What finally gave them a chance to visit Leland?"

If this seems wrong, try the challenge-test on this sentence. Remember that we tend to accept topics and, if we are inclined to challenge something, we challenge comments. In this sentence, we do not tend to challenge *that gave them a chance to visit Leland*. We would not say, "That's wrong; it was spring break that gave them a chance to visit Charlevoix." If we were to argue with the claims of this sentence, we would be more likely to challenge the mention of spring break, perhaps by saying, "No, that's wrong; it was Christmas vacation that gave them a chance to visit Leland."

Using this kind of *it*-cleft can have ethical implications, since writers may include material after the *that* that is not factual. For example, if I were to write to a dean the following about one of my students, I would have to be very careful about the facts:

> It is self-deception that has made Walter a totally irresponsible student.

Now Walter may in fact deceive himself. But do you see what I have done with the end of this *it*-cleft? I have treated the claim that he is a totally irresponsible student as a given, as a fact. So I would have to be most careful to establish this as a fact before expressing it in this position.

Why would writers reverse the general rule of expressing topics before comments? We have seen that there is much communicative sense in announcing what we will write about before we convey information about it. And that is the biggest clue here. Writers use the second kind of *it*-cleft when they can be fairly sure that their readers already have in mind what the sentence is about but are facing obstacles in understanding the comment. Thus they must make the comment clear, and they must do so quickly, so quickly that the topic must wait to be expressed. These writers are facing significant pressures.

When might this happen? When readers know that something was done but do not know which of several people or things did it.

As informal evidence for this, consider what happened to me one day last year after I got home from work. Sand from our sandbox was all over our driveway. I confronted two of my sons and three neighbor boys and asked, "Who threw the sand all over the driveway?" One of the neighbors was really saying, "It was Nicholas who threw the sand all over the driveway" when he said, "It was Nicholas." His being able to drop the *who* and everything after it shows that he knew that I was familiar with it and that it was not the point of the sentence. His main job was to pick out Nicholas from several candidates, one of whom was he.

P. D. James uses an *it*-cleft for this purpose in *Cover Her Face*. At one point, several members of the Maxie family and Detective Dalgleish are having a tense conversation. Stephen Maxie asks how his sister, who had been attacked, is doing. As readers, we strongly expect someone to answer. But since there are many suspects, some of whom may not wish to answer since a response might incriminate them, we cannot tell who it will be. Then James uses an *it*-cleft:

> It was Dalgleish who answered. . . . (p. 209)

People also use the second kind of *it*-cleft to correct mistaken views that they believe their audience has. Since speakers can tell whether their listeners have mistaken views more easily and quickly than writers can tell whether their readers have mistaken views, this function is more frequent in speech. But it is also common in writing.

Again I turn to James's *Cover Her Face* for an example. Near the end of the novel, Stephen Maxie is talking to a former employer of Sally Jupp. The employer expects Stephen to want to know more about Sally's past and to be concerned primarily with her death. But that is not the case for Stephen, and he sets things straight with an *it*-cleft:

It's the child I'm really worrying about. (p. 196)

The second kind of *it*-cleft is perhaps the best device to illustrate how a functional approach to language leads to important insights. From a functional perspective, we examine the context of the sentence, the nature of information in parts of the sentence, what the writers are apparently assuming about their readers' knowledge, and what the writers are using that information to do. When we examine the second kind of *it*-cleft in this way, we discover an elegant relationship among sentence structure, sentence meaning, sentence function, and sentence context.

Exercise Four

Turn each of the following sentences into the cleft form that is specified after it. For example, if you were asked to turn *I have sore eyes* into a *what*-cleft, you would produce *What I have is sore eyes*.

1. I would like a new bookcase. (*what*-cleft)
2. He was picking the rosebuds from the bushes near the garage. (*what*-cleft)
3. Franklin caught the first fish of the day. (*what*-cleft)
4. Henry is developing a new philosophy of education. (*what*-cleft)
5. Steve responded to those attacks on scholarship. (*it*-cleft; express *Steve* after *It was*)
6. Steve responded to those attacks on scholarship. (*it*-cleft; express *those attacks on scholarship* after *It was*)
7. Ken drove to Hardy Dam on Saturday. (*it*-cleft; express *Ken* after *It was*)
8. Ken drove to Hardy Dam on Saturday. (*it*-cleft; express *Hardy Dam* after *It was*)
9. I am really worried about their paraphrases. (*it*-cleft; express *their paraphrases* after *It is*)
10. The problem of intentionality underlies all practices of interpretation. (*it*-cleft; express *the problem of intentionality* after *It is*)

Exercise Five

Each of the following short selections of prose should be completed by either a *what*-cleft or an *it*-cleft. Complete each with the form and content that seem most appropriate. For example, if I were asked to complete the cluster, *He did not want a new truck. He did not want a new model airplane*, I would add a sentence such as *What he wanted was a new baseball.*

1. Teresa and Lyle could easily have chosen to have a large wedding with hundreds of guests. And they could have opted for a lavish reception at one of the private country clubs around town. Further, they could have decided on a honeymoon cruise around the world.

2. They argue that a writer's method of composing is the key factor in that writer's success. The method either stimulates or represses ideas. The method either facilitates or frustrates writing an early draft.

3. They asked whether I was concerned about the welfare of the student teachers. Later they wondered whether I was worried about getting my students' term papers graded. They all missed the point.

4. To this point I have reviewed the research that bears upon my experiment. I have presented in detail the materials that I used. And I have laid out the statistical design of the study.

5. Here we do not have a proposal to leave the curriculum alone. Nor do we have a proposal for some tinkering with the nature of existing courses. Further, here we do not have a proposal to rearrange systems of control over areas of the current curriculum.

Exercise Six

Each of the following short passages contains an *it*-cleft or a *what*-cleft. Describe how each form functions in its context. For example, consider the following short cluster:

> She walked to the counter and saw several different kinds of cheeses. It was cheddar that she wanted.

Here this second kind of *it*-cleft functions to pick out one kind of cheese from several possibilities.

1. This new songbook has been compiled and reviewed by a standing committee of some of the best people in the field. It is not intended to appeal to just a slice of society. It is intended to be useful for people of all ages and occupations. What we have here is a record of and a tribute to all segments of our culture.

2. A phone-type is one of all the possible sounds in a language. There are many phone-types for each language, and often the untrained person cannot hear the difference between one phone-type and one of its near relatives. A phoneme, on the other hand, is one of the significant sounds in language. This means that it is a distinction in sound that marks a distinction in meaning. Each phoneme is really made up of one or more phone-types. What we mean is that each phoneme is a set or group of similar-sounding phone-types.

3. She went into the store looking for one—and only one—thing. The salesman first tried to sell her several gallons of the paint he had on sale. Then he tried to persuade her to buy a new paint-pump and paint roller. Later still he ushered her into the hardware section and tried to get her to buy one of the special levels that he had just reduced. But none of his tactics worked. What she wanted was a roll of wallpaper.

4. In his studies in literary and music criticism, he discovered that in the nineteenth century allegory became far less popular than it had been before. His explanation was that allegory is dependent on a framework of belief that most people in a culture agree upon. And it was such a framework that collapsed under the onslaughts of skepticism and romanticism.

5. My son and I had fished for nearly two hours along the north shore of Chain Lake. We had caught some bluegills and one undersized bass, but the fish were not biting fast or hard. That led my son to complain, "But Dad, they're taking so long to bite!" It was that statement that reminded me of my days on other lakes with my father.

6. The first woman across the finish line lifted her arms in exultation but then collapsed across the ropes that guided runners through the exit chute. Several race officials were close to her, but none of them moved. They acted as if they wished she had collapsed out of their sight. It was the Grand Marshall of the race who finally helped her back to her feet and walked her to the first aid tent.

7. My students could not understand why I was upset with them. They asked whether their revisions had been superficial or sloppy. They wondered whether some people in the class had skipped their conferences with me. They even asked if I thought they had not been

alert enough in class recently. They were not close to the real cause of
my irritation. It was their apathy on campus that bothered me.

TO REVIEW:
THE IMPORTANCE OF COMMENTS

In this chapter I have shown why the main point of a sentence
should be expressed in its comment. I have also explained some
syntactic devices that call special attention to comments. The
comment, particularly the end of the comment, should provide the
information that most clearly responds to the question or concern
that motivated the sentence in the first place. In most sentences,
therefore, the topic will flow into the comment. This order is strongly
motivated by the nature of communication itself. Occasionally (as in
the second kind of *it*-cleft), the comment will precede the topic, but
there will usually be a strong or unusual rhetorical motivation for
such an ordering of elements.

In the student writing that I have seen, young writers often do not
express their most important information at the end of a sentence.
One probable reason for this is that they are not sensitive enough to
what is the most important information in their sentences. They
might become more sensitive if they were to read their prose aloud.
Then they should be able to hear where the main accents in each
sentence naturally fall. Another probable reason for their wasting
chances to express their most important information at the end of a
sentence is impatience. They have come up with that information,
do not want to forget it, and therefore hurry to include it in a
sentence. Thus they often express at the beginning of a sentence
what should be at the end. Such practice makes examining comments during revision a wise strategy.

FURTHER READING

Bolinger, D. (1952). "Linear Modification," *Publications of the Modern
    Language Association, 67,* 1117-1144.
Bolinger, D. (1957). "Maneuvering for Accent and Position," *College Com-
    position and Communication, 8,* 234-238.
Bolinger, D. (1958). "Stress and Information," *American Speech, 33,* 5-20.
Labov, W. (1986, March). "Oral Discourse and the Demands of Literacy."

Paper presented at the Conference on College Composition and Communication, New Orleans.

Prince, E. F. (1978). "A Comparison of Wh-Clefts and *It*-Clefts in Discourse," *Language, 54,* 883–906.

Smith, C. S. (1971). "Sentences in Discourse: An Analysis of a Discourse by Bertrand Russell," *Journal of Linguistics, 7,* 213–235.

Maintaining Focus and Emphasis in Longer and More Complicated Sentences

Every phrase and every sentence is an end and a beginning. . . .

—T. S. Eliot, "Little Gidding"

Swirling had a sudden flash of insight into Becky's conversational style. She was a Cubist, breaking up sentences and geometrically reassembling their grammatical components, as artists did linear, those that had subjects being denied predicates, or having them crop up elsewhere in the design, while predicates stood juxtaposed in artful divorce from their subjects.

—Peter De Vries, *Madder Music*

Most of the sentences we examined in earlier chapters were relatively short and simple. Obviously, if you were to write one such sentence after another in your essays, those essays would probably become monotonous. Moreover, often the work that you want a sentence to do in an essay will require that it be longer and more complex than many of those I have used for examples.

The English language provides us with several structures to use to add information to sentences. Some of these, however, allow us little or no choice about where we can position them in sentences. Adjective clauses, for example, typically follow the word that they modify: *Ernie's cottage, **which is on the Little Muskegon River**, was the site of their picnic.* But when you can choose where to position structures within sentences, you should place them in accordance with the principles of proper focus and emphasis that we have examined.

THE FOURTH GUIDELINE

The fourth guideline extends those principles to longer and more complex sentences: In general, with relatively long and complex sentences, make sure to express an easily identifiable topic early and your most important information on that topic as near the end as possible.

In this chapter we will examine some of the more common ways in which writers put strains on or violate this guideline. Of course, in some instances these violations are necessary. But if you were to violate this guideline often and without good reason, you would produce prose that would be very difficult to read.

DELAYED TOPICS

One of the more obvious ways to violate the fourth guideline is to delay expressing the topic. As some of my earlier examples have demonstrated, the topic will not and need not always appear first in a sentence.

Often the topic will be preceded by an adverb (*later*), a prepositional phrase (*for the same reason*), an infinitive phrase (*to assemble the bicycle*), a participial phrase (*trying to keep his head above water*), an absolute phrase (*the waves having eroded the shoreline*), a connective (*in addition*), an action marker (*I begin by noting that*), a modality marker (*perhaps*), a narrator (*Tom said that*), an attitude marker (*fortunately*), or an adverbial clause (*as we strolled down the boardwalk*), among other possibilities. In most cases, you will not need to fear that you are beginning all your sentences with the topic. Most of us regularly and quite naturally use one or more of several different elements before the topic in our sentences.

But the topic should usually appear quite early. The main reason is that it gives readers something to which to relate all the information that follows. Without such a point of reference, readers have to hold the information in a vacuum until they learn what in their memories they are to connect it to. Having to do this can put a heavy strain on their memories.

One common way to delay the topic is to place a modifying element before it. A sentence in which the modifying element delays the topic and comment quite extensively is usually called a periodic sentence. Here is a short one: *Exhausted from splitting wood in the heat of the day, Tony had to take some salt tablets.* The topic of this sentence, *Tony*, does not appear until after the introductory participial phrase.

Periodic sentences have important functions. They can create suspense. And they can convey their topic and comment with a great deal of force.

When we construct them, however, we have to be careful not to write dangling modifiers. A dangling modifier is one in which the implied subject or actor is different from the subject (and also usually the topic) of the following clause. Some of these are quite obvious and provide the material for uproarious coffee-room discussions: *Tucking my sons into their sleeping bags, a mosquito buzzed in my ears.* The introductory modifier is a dangler since its implied subject (*I*) is different from the subject that follows (*a mosquito*). As it stands, the sentence makes it seem as if the mosquito were tucking my sons into their sleeping bags. The sentence should be revised to read something like this: *As I was tucking my sons into their sleeping bags, a mosquito buzzed in my ears.*

Other dangling modifiers are neither so obvious nor so funny. Here is one from a graduate student: "When reading, knowledge from our heritage helps us perceive meaning in a text." The introductory modifier is a dangler since its implied subject (*we*) is different from the subject of the following clause (*knowledge*). This sentence should be revised to read something like this: *When we are reading, knowledge from our heritage helps us perceive meaning in a text.*

Even if we are never tempted to write a dangling modifier, we must not forget how important the early portion of our sentences is. If we use the early portion to modify a topic or a part of a comment, we are delaying the point when readers can tell what the sentence is about. In so doing we put a strain on their ability to follow our prose.

So as you edit your sentences, check them for delays of the topic. If you find yourself delaying the topic for more than a line and a half or so, you should make sure that the suspense you create or the emphasis that you end the sentence with justifies the delay. Obviously, the need for such justification grows greater the more periodic sentences you use.

What follows is a sentence in which the topic does not appear for several lines:

> Overwhelmed by the structural constraints of schools as currently organized and operated and irresistible pressures at the State and local level to deliver services without appreciable investment in their continuous evaluation and improvement, practitioners fall back on the tried and true, the old nostrums, or the patterns observed or applied to them when they were pupils themselves.
>
> (Hendrik Gideonse, *In Search of More Effective Service: Inquiry as a Guiding Image for Educational Reform in America*, p. 11)

The topic, *practitioners*, does not appear until after 33 other words. It is difficult for me to imagine a justification for this delay, since the writer does not seem to be aiming for special suspense and since, although the comment is emphatic, it is not extraordinarily so. It seems that the writer decided to express a great deal of information in one sentence and thought that a manageable way to do so would be to place much of it early. When I first read the early portion of this sentence, however, I wanted very much to know what all the information relates to, but once I found out, I discovered that I could not remember all of the introductory material.

If you find sentences such as this in your drafts and cannot justify them, how would you revise them? Perhaps your first inclination would be to move the topic to the beginning, follow it with the modifying information, and then express the main predicate at the end. You would end up with the following:

> Practitioners, overwhelmed by the structural constraints of schools as currently organized and operated and irresistible pressures at the State and local level to deliver services without appreciable investment in their continuous evaluation and improvement, fall back on the tried and true, the old nostrums, or the patterns observed or applied to them when they were pupils themselves.

This sentence probably seems almost as awkward and hard to read as the original. Although it announces its topic at the beginning, it does something else that usually causes trouble for readers: It separates its main subject from the main verb by several words. Usually it is wise not to separate the subject and the verb, or the verb and its objects or complement, by several words. With one or a few words separating the subject and the verb, no one has much trouble reading:

> Practitioners, therefore, fall back on the tried and true, the old nostrums, or the patterns observed or applied to them when they were pupils themselves.

But separating the subject and the verb by 33 words keeps readers from relating elements of the syntactic core of the sentence.

Some revisions, however, are better than the original. You could state the topic, express the modifying information in an adjective clause, and leave the end untouched:

> Practitioners, who are overwhelmed by the structural constraints of schools as currently organized and operated and irresistible pressures at the State and local level to deliver services without appreciable investment in their continuous evaluation and improvement, fall back on the tried and true, the old nostrums, or the patterns observed or applied to them when they were pupils themselves.

This is an improvement, but some readers might object that the subject is too far removed from its verb.

To meet this objection, you could try using an introductory adverbial clause. The practitioners would then be referred to once in the adverbial and once in the independent clause:

> Since practitioners are overwhelmed by the structural constraints of schools as currently organized and operated and irresistible pressures

at the State and local level to deliver services without appreciable investment in their continuous evaluation and improvement, they fall back on the tried and true, the old nostrums, or the patterns observed or applied to them when they were pupils themselves.

If this sentence seems too long and thick to you, you would have to break it up into two sentences:

Practitioners are overwhelmed by the structural constraints of schools as currently organized and operated and irresistible pressures at the State and local level to deliver services without appreciable investment in their continuous evaluation and improvement. Therefore, they fall back on the tried and true, the old nostrums, or the patterns observed or applied to them when they were pupils themselves.

Or you could divide the original into three sentences:

Practitioners are overwhelmed by the structural constraints of schools as currently organized and operated. They are also overwhelmed by irresistible pressures at the State and local level to deliver services without appreciable investment in their continuous evaluation and improvement. Therefore, they fall back on the tried and true, the old nostrums, or the patterns observed or applied to them when they were pupils themselves.

Deciding among options such as these will depend on the text into which the sentence or sentences have to fit and on your estimate of your readers' abilities to handle complex sentence structures.

Exercise One

Find whatever dangling modifiers appear in the following sentences. Then revise the sentences so that the problems are corrected.

For example, in *Driving through the Smoky Mountains, the azaleas were spectacular*, the participial phrase *Driving through the Smoky Mountains* is a dangling modifier because its implied subject (a reference to a person or some people) is different from azaleas. You could correct it as follows: *As they drove through the Smoky Mountains, they found the azaleas beautiful.*

1. Working on the word processor all morning, his eyes began to ache.
2. Driving to Ann Arbor on a warm and humid day, their air conditioner stopped working.

3. Watching the Tigers play the Blue Jays, only two balls landed near them.

4. Putting the manuscript into a manilla envelope and sending it to the mailroom, the professor felt relieved to have finished work on the book.

5. Planning to move to South Bend, their standard of living promised to improve.

Exercise Two

In the five sentences below, the topic is delayed to some extent. In each sentence, identify the topic and discuss how serious you think the delay is. If the delay strikes you as serious, revise the sentence in as many ways as you can, and discuss the advantages and disadvantages of each revision relative to the others.

For example, you might see a sentence such as this: *Thrashing around in the bottom of the boat, the muskie threatened to flip back into Munuscong Bay.* Here the topic is *the muskie.* It is delayed, but the delay does not seem serious enough to warrant a revision. What contributes to this judgment is that the modifying information helps identify the topic by narrowing the range of possibilities for it.

1. On one of those days when it is so hot that the grasshoppers seek the shade on the underside of leaves, when cattle welcome the shade of even a telephone pole, and when heat waves do their taunting dance on the horizon, workers for the county road commission decided to patch cracks in the asphalt road in front of our house.

2. Committed to the cause of free speech for all members of the country, no matter what their backgrounds and motives, and regardless of the fact that people would have to listen to or read nonsense or offensive material occasionally, the senator carefully steered the new bill through his committee.

3. In the spirit of civility that so often has characterized members of that department, who have learned that politeness and tact are the best means to achieve the ends that they all agree are of the greatest significance to the future health of their department, Professor Wanigan offered to participate in the writing-across-the-curriculum program.

4. Their hopes shattered in the realization that speed, flexibility, endurance, and other blessings of youth had stolen away, the faculty football team conceded defeat to the seniors.

5. Worried by the prospect that the professor might lose some term papers, she kept three copies of hers.

Exercise Three

In each of the following sentences the subject of the independent clause is separated from its verb by several words. Rewrite each sentence in as many ways as you can, trying to correct the problem or to lessen the severity of the problem.

For example, consider the following sentence:

Jason, after standing in the boat brazenly by himself, became scared and started to yell for help.

You could rewrite this in several ways, three of which follow:

After standing in the boat brazenly by himself, Jason became scared and started to yell for help.

After he stood in the boat brazenly by himself, Jason became scared and started to yell for help.

Jason stood in the boat brazenly by himself. Then he got scared and started to yell for help.

1. The president of the college, after thinking about the matter and consulting with the faculty parliamentarian, ruled that the amendment was out of order.
2. The young delegates, somewhat anxious about the presentation that they had agreed to make on the last night of the convention, asked to reserve a room in which they could rehearse their speeches.
3. After rumbling ominously in the distance, the thunderstorm, now with its top up around 60,000 feet and with winds in the 50–60 mile-per-hour range, blew into Otsego County.
4. Members of the women's softball team, very nervous in their appearance in post-season play and yet elated in making it to the semifinals, asked former team members to give them a pep talk.
5. The abandoned pine camp, gradually being invaded by poplars, lay with all its secrets of logging days buried deep within the moss.

LONG TOPICS

Another way in which writers violate the fourth guideline is to use very long topics. I touched on this in Chapter 4, where I noted that the trouble with long topics is that they are hard to understand in the first place and then also hard to remember. I can now add that long topics usually create long separations between the subject and verb of independent clauses. In view of these problems, in general you should take care not to make your topics too long. The necessary qualification is that sometimes fairly long topics work well and are justified. When at one point in an essay you have to refer in a topic to some information that you included long before, you might have to use a long topic to call that information back to your readers' minds with sufficient force. Or, when you are building an essay around extended comparisons or contrasts, often you will have to use longer topics to keep the compared or contrasted bits of information distinct in your readers' minds. Finally, writers frequently use longer topics toward the ends of their essays to sum up much of the material that they have already conveyed.

For instance, in the discussion section of a research report, two psychologists use the following long topic:

> "The set of analyses conducted on a small group of depressed subjects while they were still depressed, essentially a demonstration of test-retest reliability of the SRET [self-referent encoding task], revealed very consistent results."
>
> (Keith S. Dobson and Brian F. Shaw, "Specificity and Stability of Self-Referent Encoding in Clinical Depression," *Journal of Abnormal Psychology*, 1987, 96, p. 38)

This topic extends up to *revealed*, but in its context it is not overly difficult to understand, primarily because it sums up information from earlier sections of the report.

Generally, however, long topics put strains on readers. Here is an example:

> "The extremely low level of support for educational research and development nationally, given the reasonable expectations generated at the time of its expansion in the mid-sixties, especially the important steps taken to reinforce and expand the institutional framework for the conduct of educational R & D, has contributed to pre-existing squabbles that have occasionally arisen within and between the educational research community, the National Institute of Education, teacher education, and the organized profession."
>
> (Hendrik D. Gideonse, *In Search of More Effective Service*, p. 18)

Here the topic includes everything through *educational R & D*, a total of about 45 words. By the time readers finish this topic, it is difficult for them to remember it. Either before or after reading the comment, therefore, they probably have to go back through the topic to understand it. This task is difficult because the topic has some logical qualifications within it.

Techniques Commonly Used to Construct Long Topics

What are some of the more common methods used to construct long topics? I will touch on five.

One is to use a long appositive. An appositive is a word, phrase, or clause placed after a noun to modify it. If the noun the appositive modifies is part of a topic, the appositive will also be part of the topic. And if the appositive is long, obviously the whole topic will be long. Here is a topic that is long primarily because of the long appositive it contains:

> Last week the writing program proposal, the one originally written in 1982 and then ignored for two years until some changes in the administration occurred, appeared on the agenda for the approaching faculty meeting.

The easiest way to shorten this topic is to divide the sentence into two, expressing the substance of the appositive in a separate sentence with two independent clauses:

> The writing program proposal was originally written in 1982, but then it was ignored for two years until some changes in the administration occurred. Last week it appeared on the agenda for the approaching faculty meeting.

Another way writers can construct long topics is to use adjective clauses. Often writers use a noun as part of a topic and then modify it with an adjective clause: **The cottage that they wanted to buy** *was too expensive.* Usually this causes little difficulty; in fact, it is an excellent way to incorporate into one sentence information that probably does not deserve a sentence of its own.

However, when writers include several adjective clauses in one topic, they can cause trouble for readers. Consider the following sentence: *The prize that was displayed in the store that we passed on the days on which we drove to the beach that was near Grand Haven always caught Jonathan's attention.* Here everything before *always caught* is part of the topic. In addition to being hard to take in on one reading, such topics can give the impression of looseness or aimlessness as they move from one modified noun to another. Each of the modified nouns after the first in the example above moves further away from the meaning of the first. Perhaps the easiest way to shorten this topic is to transform as many of the adjective clauses as possible into participial or prepositional phrases and to omit any unnecessary adjective clauses: *The prize displayed in the store that we passed on our way to the beach near Grand Haven always caught Jonathan's attention.*

Equally troubling is that sometimes such topics include information that probably deserves to be emphasized in a comment. Consider this sentence: *The university that is renowned for the prowess of its athletic teams and that ensures that all of its athletes on scholarships graduate in at least five years does not exist.* One could make a good case that some of the information in the adjective clauses, especially that about ensuring that the athletes graduate in at least five years, belongs in the comment.

One way to do this is to move *does not exist* immediately after *The university: The university does not exist that is renowned for the prowess of its athletic teams and that ensures that all its athletes graduate in at least five years.* Or you could reword the topic and change the adjective clauses into verb phrases in the comment: *No university is renowned for the prowess of its athletic teams and ensures that all its athletes graduate in at least five years.*

Sometimes, of course, these methods of shortening topics with adjective clauses will not work, and you will have to take the adjective clause or clauses and convert them into separate sentences.

A third way in which writers construct long topics is by using long noun clauses. I suspect that experienced writers do this more often than beginning writers, but long noun clauses as topics appear occasionally in most writers' work. Most of us sometimes write sentences such as this: *That students should have the right to make recommendations to the academic council and yet not have the right to vote on matters before that council is an intolerable injustice.* Here the topic extends up to *is.* Such long topics function well in reintroducing information already included in an essay. But when this is not the case, and when you find several long noun clauses as topics in your drafts, you will probably want to revise them.

One way to do so is simply to reverse the material in the topic and the comment: *An intolerable injustice is that students have the right to make recommendations to the academic council and yet do not have the right to vote on matters before that council.* Here the topic is the short phrase *An intolerable injustice.* This revision seems to be quite an improvement, but before accepting it, you would have to make sure that this new focal point fits in with the others in the essay you are writing. This focal point would fit well with others related to injustice or student grievances.

If such is not the case and you need to maintain an order of information like that in the sentence with the noun clause as topic, you could break that sentence into two and have shorter topics: *Students have the right to make recommendations to the academic council and yet no right to vote on matters before that council. This is an intolerable injustice.* Here the two topics are very short: *Students* and *This.* One other matter to check involves the word *This.* It is dangerous to use this word (or *that, these, those,* and *such*) unless the context clarifies what it refers to. Otherwise readers might wonder whether it refers to material included in several sentences or even in whole paragraphs. In this context, though, I would judge the reference to be clear.

A fourth way writers construct long topics is by using strings of prepositional phrases. In the following sentence, the word *importance* is followed by five prepositional phrases, all of which are part of the topic: *The importance of this campaign to the college and to its constituents for the present and into the future cannot be exaggerated.* Often such a string, although conveying a kind of breathless feeling, will not cause as much trouble as some of the other constructions that we have examined.

That situation can change when the individual phrases become longer. And it almost certainly will change when the prepositions link several nominalizations into one long topic: *The termination of our analysis of students' interpretations of professors' written reactions to essays was ordered by the provost.*

To revise such a sentence, we might begin by making the passive verb active: *The provost ordered the termination of our analysis of students' interpretations of professors' written reactions to essays.* Here we have cut the original topic down to *The provost,* which we would accept, of course, only if this focal point does not clash in context.

But we could make this sentence even more readable by examining each nominalization, discovering who is doing what to whom, and then deciding how often we should substitute one of those agent-action-goal complexes for a nominalization. Going through this process produces the following: *The provost ordered us to stop analyzing how students interpret professors' written reactions to essays.* Even if your essay were to demand a focal point other than *The provost*, you could find one and still make the sentence more readable: *We had been analyzing how students interpret professors' written reactions to essays but were ordered to stop by the provost.*

Finally, we should examine one other tactic that some writers—particularly those trying to sound impressively scholarly—use to build long topics. They construct strings of nouns and modifiers and then use these strings as topics. Quite a long string functions as the topic in the following sentence: *Upper elementary school classroom management technique emphasis has led some student teachers to neglect their content-area courses.*

Sometimes such strings become well known to all who work in an area, and they take on a life of their own. These you will not need to worry about too much as long as you can be sure your readers work in the field in which the strings are known. But most noun strings are awkward to some degree. And many are ambiguous. It is difficult to tell, for example, what the word *Upper* in the example modifies.

So, generally, you should try to recast sentences with such noun strings as topics. A good way to start is to examine them from the end to the beginning. Doing this helps us see what is going on in the example: Someone is emphasizing classroom management techniques for the upper elementary school. Using this knowledge, we could write a sentence with a more understandable topic: *Emphasis on techniques for classroom management in the upper elementary school has led some student teachers to neglect their content-area courses.*

But this topic (everything through *school*) is still long and probably calls for revision. To revise it, we would have to include a reference to who we think is doing the emphasizing: *Professors are emphasizing techniques for classroom management in the upper elementary school, and that has led some student teachers to neglect their content-area courses.* This sentence has two independent clauses and therefore two topics; both of these are short: *Professors* and *that*. But since a cause-and-effect relationship lies behind this sentence, we would be wiser to make that relationship explicit by making the first clause dependent: *Since professors are emphasizing techniques for classroom management in the upper elementary school, some student teachers are neglecting their content-area courses.* This sentence is easier to read than the original, and it still begins and ends with essentially the same information that the original does.

If you follow the advice given here and make long topics shorter wherever necessary, in addition to the other benefits discussed, you will be writing in accordance with an important principle: the short-to-long principle. This holds that sentences will be more readable and graceful if they move from shorter topics to longer comments, not from longer topics to shorter comments. You would probably intuit this principle for yourself if you were to read many sentences with long noun clauses serving as topics. Apart from matters of focal points, it is clear that the first of the following two sentences moves less gracefully than the second:

> That he hoped to write a novel during his Christmas vacation was the surprise.

> The surprise was that he hoped to write a novel during his Christmas vacation.

You should also keep the short-to-long principle in mind each time you write a series. Often, of course, principles of logic or emphasis dictate the order of items in a series. You would not order the elements in a series of verb phrases like this: *He did some sit-ups, brushed his teeth, and woke up.* Logic dictates that the waking up should be mentioned first; the other two activities could be mentioned in the order they took place.

Nor would you order a series of subordinate clauses in this way: *They did not consider his short story for a prize because parts of it were plagiarized, because it lacked voice, and because it had narrow margins.* As we have seen, final position in a sentence is the position of greatest emphasis, and therefore what appears there ought to be the most important information. But the information about the narrow margins is almost certainly not the most important reason that the short story was not considered for a prize. I would express the information about plagiarism last.

When principles of logic or emphasis do not apply to the order of elements in a series, you should follow the short-to-long principle. You would write *Our new nylon tent is sturdy, rainproof, and easy to carry*, not *Our new nylon tent is easy to carry, rainproof, and sturdy*. The difference is not great, but the first builds and then ends firmly. The second ends more weakly.

Exercise Four

Revise each of the following sentences in as many ways as you can think of, always trying to produce shorter topics. Then discuss the advantages and disadvantages of each revision relative to the others, as well as the kinds of contexts into which each might fit.

For example, working with the sentence *The one who ran the fastest was Tim*, you could produce the following revision: *Tim was the one who ran the fastest*. The original would be more appropriate in a context focusing on several runners or on several runners' speeds, while the second would be more appropriate in a context focusing on Tim, Tim and his running ability, or Tim as contrasted with several others.

1. The map that he sent to us on the day that we left for the cottage that is located south of Paradise was easy to read.
2. That they would suggest that we participated in the conference for personal profit and professional advancement is outrageous.
3. Her course, the one that has attracted at least forty students each time it has been offered, now has only fifteen students enrolled in it.
4. A decision to effect the immediate termination of your employment with Faxco Incorporated has been made.
5. The new English department conference room lunch-time coffee rules irritated them daily.
6. Pendills Creek, the small stream fed by springs high on Mariners' Ridge, is home to some huge rainbow trout.
7. That they were not allowed to use the racquetball court while the convention was in progress on campus infuriated them.
8. Pervasive final examination performance anxiety affected our students last spring.
9. The best approach to handling students with deeply repressed needs for attention from teachers and other authority figures is to be firm, patient, and supportive.
10. The hotel with the best view of the lakes that stretch out to the east and the west is the Grand Hotel.

LONG AND COMPLEX COMMENTS

The third way writers can violate the fourth guideline is to construct excessively long and complex comments. If we follow the short-to-long principle, our comments will be longer than our topics. And they need to be, since they carry the essential message of sentences. Therefore, long comments will not contribute to sentence complexity as much as long topics will.

Nevertheless, we have to be careful not to pack more information into our comments than our readers can take in. Here is a sentence that is difficult to read primarily because of its long comment; the comment begins with the second word:

> Teachers need to be liberally educated in the sense that they are freed from their own parochial viewpoints, and comfortable in their knowledge of the broader historical, social, and technological context in which they work as professionals and which constitutes the backdrop for the educational goals they serve.
>
> (Hendrik Gideonse, *In Search of More Effective Service*, p. 9)

We are probably most easily tempted to write longer comments than we should by the possibility of using several verb phrases in one sentence. At one time or another, most of us have written sentences such as this: *The crane stood in the shallow water, peered into the shadows along the shore for signs of intruders, started to poke among the rushes for minnows and tadpoles, and then beat its way clumsily into the air when it sensed the hikers approaching.*

From one point of view, we could claim that this sentence has four comments (one per verb phrase), each of which could be expressed in a separate topic-comment construction with the topic of *The cranes* or *They*. But since that topic is not expressed with each verb phrase, we would have to say that everything after *The crane* is one long comment. As I noted earlier, all of us occasionally package up several potential individual comments into one long comment. Doing so can be economical, and it can create prose with a pace that mimics the pace of occurrences.

However, if you were to include several such sentences in an essay or write several in a row, you would probably create an almost breathless feeling in your prose. And readers would begin to have difficulty remembering both the information in the comments and what that information connects to.

You should get some sense of this from even the following short paragraph:

> In this book Monke tries to uncover the roots of the debate over the nature of poetic language, attempts to reveal how poetic language and metaphors are related, and takes great strides toward defining the essence of our linguistic capabilities. Some of his critics say that he argues in circles, charge him with ignoring the claims of those associated with the Prague School, and claim that he presupposes things that he never acknowledges in the book. Other critics contend that the questions Monke asks are not worth asking, and point out that discussions such as he tries to start are no longer seen as rewarding.

This paragraph has only three sentences, but since all of them pack much information into their comments, you should get an idea of how difficult it would be to read and recall the information in several such sentences in a row.

The easiest way to slow the pace of such sentences is to break them into two or more independent clauses, each with its own topic and comment. Then you would have to decide whether to connect the clauses with a period and a capital letter, a semicolon, or a comma and a coordinating conjunction.

The final sentence in the paragraph above, for example, could be rewritten as follows: *Other critics contend that the questions Monke asks are not worth asking. They point out that discussions such as he tries to start are no longer seen as rewarding.*

Or you could consider joining these two clauses with a comma and an *and*. This technique works well, but you must be cautious with it because if you use it frequently, it will lead readers to consider your style somewhat simple and immature. It can remind them of the style children often use in speech: beginning each sentence with *And then*.

Finally, you could join these two clauses with a semicolon. Writers usually reserve semicolons to connect clauses closely related in meaning. Since these two clauses make very similar points, I would consider a semicolon a good choice: *Other critics contend that the questions Monke asks are not worth asking; they point out that discussions such as he tries to start are no longer seen as rewarding.*

We can also construct long comments by using a verb phrase with several repeated elements. For instance, we can follow a verb with a string of prepositional phrases: *They hunted along the coast of northern Lake Huron, in the depths of the cedar swamps around the Tahquamenon River, in the great pine plains that extend westward from Baraga, and along the upper reaches of the Fox River in Luce County.* Usually such sentences will not be too difficult to follow. But if you judge that one of yours is packaging up too much information, you could stop after one of the prepositional phrases, start another sentence with the same topic (or a substitute for it) and verb as the first's, and then add the rest of the prepositional phrases.

It is usually more difficult to understand and remember a comment composed of a verb and several noun clauses as its objects. Consider the following: *I have noticed that the library has become more a center for social activity than one for research, that students pack up and leave campus as many as three days before official vacations, that in some classes one-quarter of the students fail to do the reading assigned to them, and that some fraternities and sororities throw parties at least four times a week.*

By the time readers finish the last *that*-clause, they probably do not remember all of the information from the earlier ones. If you think that this might be true of some of your comments, you should put a period after one or two of the noun clauses, add a connective such as *In addition,* repeat the main subject and verb, and then add the rest of the noun clauses.

While revising, you should also take a close look at your sentences that move from an independent clause into more than one adverbial clause. I am thinking of sentences such as *She did extraordinarily well on the examination, although she had been ill for several days prior to it, and despite the fact that she had not studied for more than an hour.* As we saw in Chapter 2, in the most technical sense each of these adverbial clauses has its own topic and comment. But for our purposes it is sufficient to view the adverbials as parts of a long comment following the main-clause topic. Sentences like this can ramble on to the point that it is difficult to remember the information in the independent clause. That is probably the most important information in this sentence, but it is far from the emphatic final position.

Should you then move the two adverbials before the independent clause? Doing so would move the information about the examination to the end, but it would also create a delay before readers could see the topic. However, since the adverbials include two *she*'s, which lead into the topic *she,* moving the adverbials should not cause excessive difficulty.

On the other hand, if you do not favor the move, you could put a period after the independent clause, find a substitute for *although* and *despite the fact that,* and use it to introduce a new sentence. The result would be *She did extraordinarily well on the examination. Yet she had been sick for several days prior to it and had not studied for more than an hour.* Doing this stresses the information about her performance on the examination and about her short study time. In some contexts, such emphases might be just what you need.

Exercise Five

Each of the sentences below has a relatively long comment. Revise each in as many ways as you can, and then discuss with others the advantages and disadvantages of each revision relative to the others.

For example, consider the following sentence: *The committee knew that several members of the department preferred a book with a very traditional approach to grammar and that professors in other departments demanded a common reference book to use in settling disputes about usage.* The most obvious way to revise this sentence is to break it into two: *The committee knew that several members of the department preferred a book with a very traditional approach to grammar. They also knew that professors in other departments demanded a common reference book to use in settling disputes about usage.*

You could also join these two clauses in some other ways:

. . . grammar, and they . . .

. . . grammar; they also . . .

. . . grammar; moreover, they knew. . . .

Deciding among these is difficult without a context. But since the information in the two *that*-clauses is so closely related, I would probably opt for one of the two possibilities with a semicolon. That would make for a long overall sentence, though, and you could make a good case for breaking this long sentence into two.

1. Last night members of our team had trouble hitting any pitch with some arc on it, failed to advance runners from one base to the next, misjudged several fly balls hit deep to the outfield, missed the cut-offs on long throws, and started to argue with each other over petty things.

2. They have made their pleas for help on all the major television networks, in most of the influential newspapers, on some of the leading radio stations, and by means of pamphlets that they distributed at public gatherings.

3. He wanted to start a discussion group since he thought it would help all members review important material and even though it would cut into the time available for individual study.

4. We wondered what the students' motives for asking to form a tug-of-war team were, who the members of the team would be, and who the opponents were likely to be.

5. The provost has mandated that all courses should include a final examination, that the finals should be administered during the times officially scheduled for them, and that all students should get their graded finals back within two weeks of taking them.

End Modification

In this section so far, we have examined problems associated with packing too much information into comments. To conclude this section, I would like to describe a few patterns of adding modifiers to the end of a sentence, after the most important information. These need not detract from the punch of that information; they can be used to sharpen, specify, support, exemplify, or elaborate on it. And they can produce a pleasing flow in sentences: You make your main point, let readers pause briefly at a comma, and then sharpen that point up a bit. Doing this can add to the punch of the most important information.

Some of these modifiers are single words and short constructions. To the end of a sentence we can add adjectives (among which are participles):

> She took a called third strike, angry and embarrassed.

We can add prepositional phrases:

> Professor Mandan suddenly stopped his lecture, before the end of the hour and for no apparent reason.

We can add participial phrases:

> The trout swam straight at me, trying to create slack in the line.

We can add infinitive phrases:

> He had trained for the race for two years, to excel, to win, to set a new record.

And we can add absolute phrases:

> Dawn took the hand-off from Jo, her arm extended, her fingers stretched out to grasp the baton.

And, of course, we can combine several of these elements.

Others of these modifiers are somewhat more complex structures. One of these uses a noun phrase to sum up some information from the preceding comment and then modifies that noun phrase with an adjective clause. For example, *We worked for two days on the details of that proposal, a process that exhausted all of us.* Here the noun phrase *a process* refers to the working for two days, and the adjective clause *that exhausted all of us* adds information about that process.

Another of these structures repeats a word from the preceding material and then adds some information about it: *Joel insisted that he wanted the red bicycle, a bicycle that we could not afford,* or *They were utterly confused, confused about why students refused to submit poems for the fine arts contest.*

Of course, if you were to make one of these modifiers quite long, it might function less to sharpen readers' focus on the preceding information than to obscure it. And as with all slightly unusual structures in writing, you should not overdo the use of any of these. Read accomplished writers to see how they use end modifiers. If you use end modifiers with comments that can appropriately be sharpened or elaborated on, I would say that readers encountering such a modifier every other page or so will not think that you are overdoing it. In fact, the end modifiers will probably lead them to view your style as mature and skillful.

Exercise Six

Try to add several different kinds of end modifiers to each of the following sentences. For example, you could change I finished the fifty push-ups into I finished the fifty push-ups, wheezing, coughing, wondering what had made me think I could become a pole-vaulter. Or you could change it into I finished the fifty push-ups, exercises that I used to do using only one arm.

1. On Saturday morning they proofread six chapters of the detective novel they had collaborated on.
2. The four six-year-olds played checkers for five hours.
3. In September the colors on the hillsides around Dead Man's Cliff were spectacular.
4. Someone smashed all the cormorant eggs on Beaver Island.
5. The ferry was towed to Owen Sound for repairs.
6. A dust devil swept across Sawtooth Prairie.
7. She had decided to become a psycholinguist.
8. They conspired together and boycotted the bran muffins.
9. The sand dunes are gradually enveloping the stately beech trees.
10. The otter swam regally around the old beaver pond.

PROBLEMS WITH ADVERBIAL CLAUSES

Finally, writers can violate the fourth guideline by misusing adverbial clauses. Many adverbials convey one of two kinds of information: either background information—that which is not central to the development of an essay—or information that has already been included in the essay.

For example, in the sentence *Although dumping taconite pellets into Lake Superior was an inexpensive way to get rid of them, the pollution this practice caused was widespread and dangerous*, the adverbial conveys information that is not central and will not be developed. We can be virtually certain that the writer will go on to develop ideas about the dangerous pollution.

In the following, the adverbial clause that introduces the second sentence carries information that is included in the sentence immediately preceding it:

> Whether or not we pursue such knowledge depends, as Wayne Booth has noted, on whether we find the experience of understanding desirable. . . .
>
> If we do find it desirable, then we may be inclined to set value in a method of inquiry that views the relation between speech occasion and discourse as that between question and answer.
>
> (Jeffrey Porter, "The Reasonable Reader: Knowledge and Inquiry in Freshman English," *College English, 49*, March, 1987, pp. 342–343)

In these lights I see writers making two kinds of errors. First, sometimes they do not subordinate background or repeated information. Occasionally I find sequences of sentences such as this: *I ran out of typing paper around 4 p.m. and decided that I should go to the bookstore before supper for more. I went to the bookstore, but I found that it was all sold out of typing paper.* Most of the information in the first clause of the second sentence is expressed or implied in the first sentence. If you doubt this, read the sentences with the first clause of the second sentence omitted. We sense that nothing important is missing, which would be unlikely if the omitted information were not recoverable from the preceding sentence. Another bit of evidence here is that many people would substitute *there* for *to the bookstore*. Such substitutions usually occur only with repeated information.

Therefore, if you wish to include in the second sentence the information about going to the bookstore, you should express it in an adverbial clause: *But when I got there, I found that it was all sold out of typing paper.*

Deciding whether to include the information carried by the adverbial clause depends primarily on how much help you think readers will need in connecting these two sentences. Another consideration, though, is that retaining the adverbial adds a touch of suspense to the second sentence; the adverbial delays for a moment and sets us up to wonder about what the writer found in the bookstore.

The second kind of error with adverbials that I see, the one that violates the fourth guideline more seriously, is that writers sometimes express adverbials carrying repeated information at the end of their sentences. Such sentences do not conclude with their most important information but end weakly with information the reader already knows.

We can change the two sentences we examined above to illustrate this kind of flaw: *I ran out of typing paper at 4 p.m. and decided that I should go to the bookstore before supper for more. But I found that the bookstore was all sold out of typing paper when I got there.* And here is a sentence from a research report that exhibits this same flaw, albeit somewhat more subtly:

> Furthermore, in our study, the same negative relationship was found across several organizations, after we had controlled for other individual and organizational influences.
>
> (Charles R. Greer and Mary Anne Dorland Castro, "The Relationship Between Perceived Unit Effectiveness and Occupational Stress: The Case of Purchasing Agents," *The Journal of Applied Behavioral Science*, 1986, 22, p. 171)

I wrote that this sentence exhibits the error more subtly since the information in the final adverbial does not appear explicitly before. But in the context of a research report, information about controls is a given, is assumed. And obviously this information is not as important as that about finding the same negative relationship in several organizations. Therefore, this sentence should be revised so that the adverbial, perhaps combined with the "in our study," precedes the independent clause.

Sentences with repeated information in final adverbials are easy to produce in first drafts. But they should be revised. As you check your drafts, you should identify such adverbials and decide whether your readers will need or appreciate the connecting help that they offer. If you decide you should include them, do so—but do so at or near the beginning of your sentences.

Does this mean that no adverbial clause should ever appear at the end of a sentence? No. Some of them carry information that is not background or repeated information. In fact, some of them carry information that writers wish to stress or develop.

This may surprise you, particularly if you have read or heard that adverbial clauses (as well as adjective and noun clauses) subordinate information or show that it is less important than that in main clauses. In general, this is a valid view, one that probably rests on realizations that many adverbial clauses convey background or repeated information.

But it is wrong to assume that no adverbial clause deserves to appear in final position. In this discussion it would be better to use the other name for adverbial clauses: dependent, not subordinate, clauses. They rely on independent clauses to make full sense. If you were to hear *if you take another step*, you would wonder what would happen if you were to take another step; the clause does not make full sense by itself.

In English we often choose to make aspects of logical relationships such as conditions or causes dependent on the meaning and logic of independent clauses for their full interpretation. These are matters more of logic and grammar than of rhetorical emphasis. Therefore, these causes or conditions could still be the most important information in a sentence.

For example, it is not at all incredible that an outlaw in a Western movie would say "I'll shoot if you take another step!" The outlaw is stressing information about taking another step. That is what the hearer had better pay close attention to.

Similarly, about a year ago an editor for a major publishing firm sent me a letter that concluded this way: "I'll be happy to send you an examination copy of this textbook if you write and ask for it." Was this order of information arbitrary? Could she just as well have written, "If you write and ask for it, I'll be happy to send you an examination copy of this textbook"? I do not think so. Her sentence stresses my writing and asking for a copy of the book. And I believe that that is precisely what she wanted to stress. Sending out examination copies is a costly venture, and she probably wanted to send them only to those who wanted one and would be likely to take a close look at it.

Often you have to consider the context that you have built up when deciding whether an adverbial should go early or late in a sentence. You should write *The price is $1,800 if you want air conditioning* if in context you are stressing information about kinds and features of equipment. On the other hand, you should write *If you want air conditioning, the price is $1,800* if in context you are stressing prices.

In sum, adverbial clauses deserve careful attention. You should make sure that you express your background or repeated information in them. You should check that you do not leave adverbials carrying background or repeated information at the ends of your sentences. Finally, you should be assured that adverbials which do not carry background or repeated information might very well provide the information you want to stress in a sentence.

Exercise Seven

Revise the following paragraph according to the principles we have just examined governing the use and placement of adverbial clauses. You might find independent clauses that should be omitted or converted into dependent clauses, adverbial clauses that appear at the end of sentences but should not, and adverbial clauses that do not appear at the end of sentences but should. You might also find adverbial clauses appearing where they should.

1. The members of the English department went through several steps in selecting students for departmental awards last spring. First, the chairman asked the secretary to obtain from the registrar the names of all English majors with a grade-point average above 3.0. The secretary obtained this information, and then she circulated a list of these names to all the members of the department. They were to make notes about the English majors whom they had had in class once they received the lists. Then all the members of the department met to discuss the candidates. The meeting started somewhat chaotically. Many of the professors simply started to praise all the majors on the list that they had had once the meeting started. Since they had to make a decision during the short meeting, the chair asked for proposals for more efficient ways to handle business. Some of her colleagues suggested that they nominate students for one award at a time. To this proposal all the others agreed. If they proceeded in this way, they thought, they could finish their business in the allotted time. Therefore, the chair asked for nominations for the award for scholarship. Surprisingly, for this award only three nominations were made, and almost all members of the department voted for one of the three candidates. They voted for one, and then they moved on to nominate students for the award for creative writing. The process continued to go smoothly, and soon the professors were pleased to find that their work was finished.

TO REVIEW:
MAINTAINING FOCUS AND EMPHASIS
IN LONGER AND MORE COMPLEX SENTENCES

In this chapter we have seen that as you write longer and more complex sentences, if you are not careful, you can make it difficult for readers to focus on your topics and to recall the information from your comments. You can do this if you (1) delay presenting topics, (2) write long and complicated topics, (3) write long and complicated comments, and (4) express adverbial clauses carrying repeated information at the ends of sentences. As we examined such sources of potential difficulty, we also examined the principles of not introducing a great deal of information between the major syntactical elements of sentences (the subject, verb, and objects or complement), and of moving sentences from shorter to longer elements. All of these guidelines or principles serve only as general touchstones, and you will probably not want to follow them all of the time. But when you do not, you should be clear about the effect you are trying to achieve and the reason you are trying to achieve it.

FURTHER READING

Halliday, M. A. K. (1985). *An Introduction to Functional Grammar*. London: Edward Arnold.

Thompson, S. A. (1985). "Grammar and Written Discourse: Initial Versus Final Purpose Clauses in English," *Text, 5*, 55–84.

Tomlin, R. S. (1985). "Foreground-Background Information and the Syntax of Subordination," *Text, 5*, 85–122.

Williams, J. M. (1985). "Controlling Sprawl," *Style: Ten Lessons in Clarity and Grace* (2nd ed.). Glenview, IL: Scott, Foresman.

Winterowd, W. R. (1981) *The Contemporary Writer, a Practical Rhetoric* (2nd ed.). New York: Harcourt Brace Jovanovich, Inc.

7

Controlling Topical Progressions in Essays

"I read in the Sun that kids feel disconnected. How can that be? Connections lying over the land like stardust. They live in the Land of Nod."
> —Alice Venable Middleton in
> William Least Heat Moon's Blue Highways

Form is what interests everyone and fortunately it is wherever you are and there is no place where it is not.
> —John Cage

It is the unpremeditated and evidently habitual arrangement of his [the educated man's] words, grounded on the habit of foreseeing, in each integral part, or (more plainly) in every sentence, the whole that he then intends to communicate.
> —Samuel Taylor Coleridge, The Friend

In every work one part must be for the sake of others. . . .
> —Samuel Johnson, "Milton," in Lives of the Poets

As you read the following paragraph, judge how clear and readable it is, and try to formulate reasons for your judgment.

Recently critics have assailed the many flaws that they see in the typical American high school. A lack of motivation for academic pursuits characterizes most students. Discovering the minimum amount of work needed to graduate appears to be their goal. Having to teach many subjects with which they are unfamiliar is the task facing many teachers. In addition, little control over teaching methods is possible for them; decisions about methods are made by administrators who sometimes have been out of the classroom for as long as twenty years. As a result, the early retirement incentives offered by some states in the past few years have lured some of the ablest teachers into retirement. Lack of parental support for educational programs is another problem facing some school districts. Thus it is not surprising that in recent years funding proposals in many school districts have been defeated by the parents and their neighbors. The situation is desperate. In the near future, radical reforms will have to be undertaken in the American high school.

Most people judge this paragraph to be somewhat unclear and difficult to read. When I ask them to give reasons for their judgment, many note that some of the sentences are long. Those who have read about style or composition point out that the paragraph has many passive verbs as well as some nominalizations (*decisions*, for example).

Would you add anything to the list? You can probably guess that I am moving toward a point about sentence topics. If you examine the topics of the main clauses here, you will be reminded of a point from Chapter Six, since some topics are long and complicated (*the early retirement incentives offered by some states in the past few years*).

But here I want to examine a different source of difficulty in prose. If you have not already done so, look at the set of topics in this paragraph. To do this, identify all the topics of independent clauses and write them down, one below another. You should come up with a list close to this:

    critics
    A lack of motivation for academic pursuits
    Discovering the minimum amount of work needed to graduate
    Having to teach many subjects with which they are unfamiliar
    little control over teaching methods
    decisions about methods
    the early retirement incentives offered by some states in the past few
        years
    Lack of parental support for educational programs
    funding proposals in many school districts
    The situation
    radical reforms

When the topics are displayed in this way, I hope that my point becomes obvious. This paragraph has no consistent focal point. A few of these topics are closely related to each other, but many are not. The members of this set of topics jump around. When this happens in parts of essays or throughout essays, the essays become very difficult to read. Instead of adding information at one point or at several closely related points in their memory, readers have to focus on many different points and add information to them.

You may object that this paragraph might be written for educators, for whom all of these topics would probably be quite closely related. Perhaps that is true. Perhaps educators would find a consistent framework within which to view these topics. But I would argue that with some rewriting, this paragraph would lose nothing essential and would become much easier to read, for educators as well as for others. And I would regard that as a virtue.

For example, if we rework this paragraph and focus primarily on the school and the people closely related to it (the students, teachers, and parents) at the same time that we try to keep most other elements the same, the paragraph becomes significantly easier to read:

> Recently the American high school has been assailed by critics for many flaws. Most students have little motivation for academic pursuits. They appear to want to discover the minimum amount of work needed to graduate. Teachers have to teach many subjects with which they are

not familiar. In addition, they have little control over teaching methods; administrators who have been out of the classroom for as long as twenty years make decisions about methods. As a result, many of the ablest teachers have been lured into retirement by the early retirement incentives offered by some states in the past years. Parents fail to support educational programs. Thus it is not surprising that in recent years the parents and their neighbors have defeated funding proposals in many school districts. The situation is desperate. In the near future, the American high school will have to undergo some radical reforms.

If you were to pull the topics out of this paragraph, you would find that they make up a much more coherent set than those from the first paragraph do. And this change in topics is primarily responsible for the greater clarity and coherence of the second paragraph.

I can illustrate this point about topics in a slightly different way. One of the following paragraphs is from William Least Heat Moon's *Blue Highways*. The other I wrote, primarily by rearranging information within the sentences of the original. Which do you think is which?

Two Steller's jaybirds stirred an argy-bargy in the ponderosa. They shook their big beaks, squawked and hopped and swept down the sunlight toward Ghost Dancing [the author's vehicle] and swooshed back into the pines. They didn't shut up until I left some orts from breakfast; then they dropped from the branches like ripe fruit, nabbed a gobful, and took off for the tops of the hundred-foot trees. The chipmunks got in on it too, letting loose a high peal of rodent chatter, picking up their share, spinning the bread like pinwheels, chewing fast.

An argy-bargy was stirred by two Steller's jaybirds in the ponderosa. Ghost Dancing was the object of the shaking of their big beaks, their squawking and hopping, their swooping down the sunlight and swooshing back into the pines. I left some orts from breakfast in order to shut them up; the tops of the hundred-foot trees were their destinations as they dropped from the branches like ripe fruit, nabbed a gobful, and took off. A high peal of rodent chatter was heard as the chipmunks got in on it too, picking up their share, spinning the bread like pinwheels, chewing fast.

I hope that deciding was easy. The first paragraph is the one written by Least Heat Moon. You should have found it easier to read and more coherent than the second. And I would say that the main reason for this lies in the nature of its topics. If you line up the topics of the independent clauses in the first paragraph, you get a coherent set:

Two Steller's jaybirds
They
They
they
the chipmunks

The focus in this paragraph is on the jaybirds and the chipmunks. That focus is consistent with Moon's purpose here: to let readers know what woke him up after a night in a campground in California.

On the other hand, if you line up the topics from the second paragraph, you get the following list:

An argy-bargy
Ghost Dancing
I
the tops of the hundred-foot trees
A high peal of rodent chatter

These topics can scarcely be thought of as forming a coherent set. This group reveals quite clearly why you might well have wondered what was going on in the second paragraph. Without a consistent focus, it seems to have no point or purpose. Its writer seems to be unsure of what he wants to accomplish with it.

THE FIFTH GUIDELINE

The foregoing discussion leads into the fifth guideline: In general, try to make the topics of sentences in your essays a coherent set.

In other words, try to provide your readers with a consistent focal point as they move through your essays. Try to keep them from being jarred or surprised as they move from one topic to the next. This means that, typically, your topics should be identical to each other, closely related to each other, derivable from prior material in your essay, or associated with the same scenario (for example, an essay dealing with skiing could justifiably topicalize snow without having mentioned it earlier). In this way, sentences in parts of an essay or in the whole essay will be about identical, closely related, or previously mentioned things.

Following this guideline can probably do as much as anything else to help you achieve clarity and coherence in your writing. And examining the sets of topics that you establish can be a good way to get an idea about the kinds of overall structures that you have built up in essays.

Exercise One

Examine the sentence topics in each of the following paragraphs. Tell if you think the set of topics is satisfactorily coherent or not.

1. The real University, he said, has no specific location. It owns no property, pays no salaries and receives no material dues. The real University is a state of mind. It is that great heritage of rational thought that has been brought down to us through the centuries and which does not exist at any specific location. It's a state of mind which is regenerated throughout the centuries by a body of people who traditionally carry the title of professor, but even that title is not part of the real University. The real University is nothing less than the continuing body of reason itself.

   (Robert M. Pirsig, *Zen and the Art of Motorcycle Maintenance*, p. 143)

2. March geese are a different story. Although they have been shot at most of the winter, as attested by their buckshot-battered pinions, they know that the spring truce is now in effect. They wind the oxbows of the river, cutting low over the now gunless points and islands, and gabbling to each sandbar as to a long-lost friend. They weave low over the marshes and meadows, greeting each newly melted puddle and pool. Finally, after a few *pro-forma* circlings of our marsh, they set wing and glide silently to the pond, black landing-gear lowered and rumps white against the far hill. Once touching water, our newly arrived guests set up a honking and splashing that shakes the last thought of winter out of the brittle cattails. Our geese are home again!

   (Aldo Leopold, *A Sand County Almanac*, p. 20)

3. For an example, let us take two famous poetic parodies which appear at first sight to be diametrically opposite to each other in purpose. One is a miniature Greek epic poem called *The Battle of Frogs and Mice*, apparently written in the fifth century B.C. by an author now unknown. The other is a satirical narrative in English verse called *The Vision of Judgment*, written by Lord Byron in 1821. One is light and flimsy, the other rich and thoughtful. They both have one virtue which is not common among parodies: they are amusing even if you do not know the originals which they are satirizing.

(Gilbert Highet, The Anatomy of Satire, p. 80)

4. Topic chains are very important to the coherence of prose paragraphs. For many years now, linguists have studied them. It seems that skilled writers know almost instinctively how to move from one sentence topic to the next. Some theories of language acquisition hold that the ability to write good sentences is innate. But the environment is held up as the root cause by other theorists. Whatever is the cause, good grades usually go to essays with coherent sets of sentence topics. It appears that teachers practice what they preach when they grade compositions.

5. The glass that was then so much in demand came in two types, according to whether it was needed for small lattice windows or larger frames. The latter used broad glass; this was blown into a cylinder when molten, then the glass cylinder was split down one side and, still hot, rolled flat. The other type of glass was crown, and was made by blowing a bubble of molten glass on the end of a blowpipe. The bubble was then fixed to the end of an iron rod, the blowpipe connection was cut, and the rod was spun so that the bubble widened and flattened under the effect of centrifugal force. The flat, circular plate was then broken off the end of the rod. This kind of glass can still be seen in older houses, where it is identifiable by the familiar bull's-eye at its centre where it was connected to the rod.

(James Burke, Connections, p. 164)

TOPICAL PROGRESSIONS IN ESSAYS

Probably the easiest way to create a coherent set of topics in parts of essays or in entire essays is to control the progression of topics

from one sentence to the next. There are several common progressions in English. That is, there are several common relationships
between one topic (or occasionally its comment) and the next. I will
describe six of these here. And I will describe them in their pure
forms; in actual essays they often lose this purity. If you were to use
these progressions individually or in combinations, you would
virtually guarantee yourself a coherent set of topics in your writing.
And a coherent set of topics virtually ensures a coherent essay.

The Parallel Progression

The first progression is easy to understand. In it, the topic of one
sentence is identical or closely related to the topic of the next:

> In a word, the students [at Harvard in 1815] learned to think.
> Moreover, they learned to write.
>
> (Van Wyck Brooks, *The Flowering of New England*, p. 43)

Sometimes this progression provides the basic framework for
entire paragraphs, with one topic expressed or implied in all the
independent clauses. In each clause in the following paragraph, we
focus on Richard Wagner or something closely associated with him:

> He was an undersized little man, with a head too big for his body—a
> sickly little man. His nerves were bad. He had skin trouble. It was
> agony for him to wear anything next to his skin coarser than silk. And
> he had delusions of grandeur.
>
> (Deems Taylor, "The Monster," *Of Men and Music*)

As you can see, the parallel progression is helpful when you have
to examine any one thing—an object, an action, an event, a
person—at length. Thus it turns up often in descriptions, in
character analyses, in explanations of processes and methods, even
in narratives when one person is the focus of attention for several
sentences.

When I first acquaint my students with the parallel progression,
some of them are a bit wary of it. In the past they have been told that
they should vary the structures they use to begin sentences,
sometimes to the point that they begin each sentence differently
from those around it. Thus they see the parallel progression as a
threat to the variety they seek in sentence openings.

I respond by saying that, although I think the advice to vary
sentence openings is somewhat overplayed today and can lead to

poor prose if students vary sentence beginnings without good reason, I think it is good to keep it in mind. But using a parallel progression of topics does not have to lead to monotony in sentence openings. As we saw early in Chapter Six, topics do not always come first in sentences. Therefore, each of several sentences in a row could begin differently from all the others, but all of their topics could be in a parallel progression.

Progression from a Split Topic

This progression is a slight variation on the first. Here the topic of one sentence actually includes references to two (or more) things. One of these then becomes the topic of the second sentence. And the other becomes the topic of the third (or a later) sentence.

Stephen Jay Gould provides a good example:

> Lyell and Wallace both preached a form of preparation; virtually all builders of picket fences have done so. Lyell depicted an earth in steady-state waiting, indeed almost yearning, for the arrival of a conscious being that could understand and appreciate its sublime and uniform design. Wallace, who turned to spiritualism later in life, advanced the more common claim that physical evolution had occurred in order, ultimately, to link pre-existing mind with a body capable of using it. . . .
>
> ("In the Midst of Life . . .," *The Panda's Thumb*, p. 138)

Progression from a Hypertopic

This progression, too, is closely related to the parallel progression. In this one, generally one of two things happens. First, the topic of one sentence can be a general term. Topics of later sentences then express specific correspondents to that general term. For example:

> Problems with the traditional approach to composition instruction abound. One of these is that students get little help coming up with ideas. Another is that they learn to think that their own prose will never be as good as that of the samples from the professional writers that they study. And a third problem is that in this approach revision tends to mean only a tidying up.

Second, the topic of one sentence names something that embraces many different parts or aspects. These are not explicitly stated, but readers with the proper background knowledge would almost assume that they are parts of what the hypertopic names.

For instance, a writer of a travel brochure could make *Colorado* or *the attractions of Colorado* a hypertopic and then go on to use phrases such as *the Rocky Mountains, the Colorado River, the excellent trout streams,* and *the famous ghost towns* as topics for subsequent sentences. All these refer to things that are parts of the state of Colorado, and for this reason readers would find them closely related to the hypertopic.

The Chaining Progression

In this progression, the comment (or part of it) of one sentence carries over to become the topic of the next sentence. If the progression continues, the comment (or part of it) of the second sentence becomes the topic of the third sentence.

As indicated, this progression might govern just two sentences:

> In 1960, Americans spent, according to the only available government estimate, $1.6 billion on funerals, setting thereby a new national and world record. The $1.6 billion is, as we shall see, only a portion of what was actually spent on what the death industry calls the "care and memorialization of the dead."
>
> (Jessica Mitford, *The American Way of Death*, p. 31)

At other times, this progression governs more than two sentences, and the chain-like linkage becomes even more apparent:

> The "coherent deformation" points to the existence of a system of equivalences underlying the text. This system is to a large extent identical to what we earlier called aesthetic value. The aesthetic value is that which is not formulated by the text and is not given in the overall repertoire.
>
> (Wolfgang Iser, *The Act of Reading*, p. 82)

Sometimes writers use the chaining progression to frame major junctures. They end a section with a sentence that moves from A to B. Then they begin the next section with a sentence that moves from B to C. Doing this allows them to introduce in a prominent position (at the end of a section) the information designated by the B and to set readers up to wait expectantly for more details about it at the start of the next section.

The chaining progression is a kind of counter to the parallel progression. With the parallel progression, writers focus in each sentence on the same topic. With the chaining progression, writers move on to material that they have touched on only once before. This kind of movement makes the chaining progression well suited for analysis, logical argument, and exploration of connections among things. This movement is what people probably have in mind when they use the term *chain of reasoning*. But this movement has its limits. If writers were to follow it without exception throughout long parts of essays, they would probably end up unacceptably far away from the point at which they started.

Progression from a Split Comment

This progression is a variation on the chaining progression. Here a sentence moves from a topic to a comment in which two or more closely related things are mentioned. Then one of these becomes the topic of the next sentence. And the other becomes the topic of the third or a later sentence. For example:

> The senator spent the day talking to laid-off steelworkers and residents of a nursing home. The steelworkers complained that the practice of importing foreign steel had cost them their jobs. The nursing-home residents expressed grave concerns about the future of the social security program.

Progression from a Hypercomment

Finally, we come to a progression that works as the two kinds of progression from a hypertopic do. In this progression, a sentence's comment either includes a general term from which specific correspondents are drawn to serve as topics for later sentences, or the comment includes a reference to a whole with many necessary or probable parts.

The example I used to illustrate the first kind of progression from a hypertopic could be adjusted to serve as an example of the first kind of progression from a hypercomment. We would have to revise the first sentence so that the general term from which specific references are drawn appears not in the topic but in the comment. We would change *Problems with the traditional approach to composition abound* into *The traditional approach to composition has several problems.*

Similarly, the example that I used for the second kind of progression from a hypertopic could also be adapted to serve as an example of the second kind of progression from a hypercomment. The writer would simply have to express *Colorado* or *the attractions of Colorado* not in the topic of the first sentence but in the comment: *Tourists will find much to enjoy in Colorado.*

These six progressions are probably the most common means to link the topic or comment of one sentence to the topic of the next. Of course, if you were to examine an essay you have written, you should not expect all the connections between your sentences to be identical to one of these. Not all connections are described here. Moreover, all writers face moments when they have to introduce material that is only loosely or tangentially connected to what has gone before. Readers expect this to happen, particularly at major junctures in essays and books.

But in the main the six progressions laid out here should help you describe the linkages between most sentences in coherent essays. No writer follows any one linkage to the exclusion of all the others. Rather, writers mix and combine them to suit their purposes. In the following selection, for example, Owen Chadwick mixes instances of the parallel progression; of the parallel progression started, interrupted, then started up again; of the chaining progression; and of the progression from a split topic:

All his life Froude admired Newman. He thought him a genius and remembered what he owed. But Newman was a friend of Hurrell and Hurrell was prison. Tom Mozley, who lived briefly on an Oriel staircase with Froude, guessed that he felt the same necessity for self-assertion against Newman as against his father and Hurrell. Newman taught him that reason always ended in doubt, that on rational grounds the atheist philosophers were unanswerable, that religious truth was known through conscience, that reason must be surrendered. Froude put into Sutherland's mouth an overdrawn onslaught upon Newman's idea of faith. Faith, when so sceptical of reason that it turned into credulity, was Froude's target. He seemed to be defending his scruples by saying, "If you do not choose honest doubt you must choose popery." Two ways are set before you. One is Rome, the other Infidelity. Newman and Ward dared to use the dilemma to prove the Catholic faith. Froude used the same dilemma as a pit of waste and destruction. Either you credit the incredible or you end in moral ruin.

(*The Victorian Church*, p. 537)

Will sticking to these progressions and their near-relatives guarantee coherence for your essays? Unfortunately, no. Coherence involves more than word linkages from topics and comments to later topics. For example, how coherent would you judge the following paragraph to be?

> Our neighbors recently bought a new car. Moreover, the car that the Pope rode in when he visited Chicago was dark blue. Blue was the candidate's mood when he learned that he would not get a college teaching job. Jobs were discussed at a national labor convention in July. July has thirty-one days. Finally, days seem to grow shorter as one grows older.

It is difficult for me to imagine that anyone would find this paragraph coherent. It gives some appearance of coherence. There are clear linkages between words in adjacent sentences (the paragraph seems to be dominated by the chaining progression), and the paragraph includes some connectives (*Moreover, Finally*), which usually signal coherence quite strongly.

But in any real sense it is grossly incoherent. Why? For one thing, some words (such as *car*) are used to refer to different things. And in most coherent prose, a word used repeatedly refers to the same thing or to similar things. More important, though, this paragraph seems to fit no overall intention and situation. It is difficult to imagine a writer being able to accomplish a purpose (other than to confuse readers) in a real situation with prose such as this. In fact, if I were asked what reasonable purpose such a paragraph could serve, I would have a very difficult time coming up with an answer.

This point about an overall intention is critical. Recently a student submitted this paragraph to me:

> Greg is about six feet tall, with two-toned, curly hair, really blond on top, gradually getting darker toward the bottom. He isn't someone a girl would stop on the street and say, "Wow! Are you gorgeous!" Then again, he wouldn't be called ugly either. In the film we see that Greg has a very deep love for Peege. Even though seeing her old is very difficult for him, his love is still as strong as when he was growing up.

One could say that the structure of this paragraph is dominated by the parallel progression of topics. Most of the sentences focus on Greg or his characteristics. But notice the comments that are added to the topics. The first few have to do with Greg's appearance, but the last ones have to do with his love for Peege. They do not go together well; one wonders what they are doing in the same paragraph.

We could say, therefore, that a piece of prose could have identical or related topics and yet be incoherent, since the comments added to these topics do not go well together. And the reason they do not is that they do not work together to achieve a purpose; they do not help support a more general statement such as "Greg's love for Peege remained strong." Is the writer trying to describe Greg's appearance or his love for Peege? Or is she somehow using remarks about Greg's appearance to reveal things about his love? Looking at the paragraph, we cannot tell. Even if this paragraph were divided into two paragraphs, one focusing on Greg's appearance and one focusing on Greg's love for Peege, without a skillful transition between them, we would wonder why the one follows the other. Probably the kindest explanation of the genesis of this paragraph is that its writer intended to comment on Greg's love for Peege but used some details about his appearance first, most likely because she felt a need to introduce him gradually. Maybe, however, she was simply trying to add words to her essay.

In sum, then, I would advise you to try to link your sentences as often as possible with the progressions we have examined. But remember that this practice will work toward fundamental coherence only if you are clear about what task you have to accomplish in writing and about the situation that task will take place in.

One final caution about this advice on topical progressions: As with some of my earlier advice, you are probably wisest to follow it primarily as you revise and edit. For some people, thinking about topical progressions can get in the way as they try to come up with ideas and make early decisions about how to organize them.

Exercise Two

In the following groups of sentences, identify the kind of progression that characterizes the movement from the topic or comment of one sentence to the topic of the next. In each group, you may find examples of only one progression or of two or more progressions. For example, consider *He wanted directions to Wabasis Lake. It was supposed to be in the northeast corner of the county.* These sentences are marked by the chaining progression, with *Wabasis Lake* and *It* providing the linkage.

1. Wisconsin is a lovely state to visit. The dairy farms set amid the rolling hills are beautiful. The beaches are vast and uncrowded. And the lakes region provides dozens of recreational opportunities.
2. Her book was published last spring. It investigates the relationships between plants and poetry in seventeenth-century England.
3. They have submitted their manuscript to a major university press. The press should decide in the next week whether or not to publish it.
4. Most of his work has been on the writings of Trilling and Abrams. Trilling's work caught his attention when he was in graduate school. And Abrams' writing has recently become very helpful to him.
5. Porcupines and raccoons are their main pests. Porcupines eat the shingles on the roof of their garage. Raccoons overturn their garbage can every night.
6. He finally felt compelled to reject what is known as New Criticism. The attention to structure did not disturb him. But the stress on the literary work as a self-contained world contradicted his basic beliefs.
7. He has proposed to translate a Frisian novel. It is about a young boy's longing to go to sea. It is entitled *A Dike Too High*.
8. Every day he walks around the auditorium. He averages approximately three miles a day. This distance is great enough to get his pulse up to a brisk rate.
9. Tim likes to fish the Thornapple and the Rogue Rivers. The Thornapple is full of bass. Most of them hide in eddies just below fallen trees. The Rogue is a good river for brown trout. The big ones are a challenge for anyone to catch.
10. London will be her home and place of work next year. The productions of Shakespeare and Jonson there are especially good. And the libraries have offered her access to several rare documents.

Exercise Three

Create clusters of sentences that could serve as examples of the six kinds of progressions and of two or three combinations of progressions. You may write the clusters of sentences about whatever you like. For example, the following cluster exemplifies the chaining progression: *Her favorite novel is "Pride and Prejudice." It is full of intensely interesting characters. The most appealing of these is Elizabeth.*

Exercise Four

We can learn some valuable lessons from writing sentences according to formulas and by trying to make the sentences *incoherent*. Try to do that with the following formulas. In some cases the words you use to link topics or comments to later topics should refer to different things. In other cases you could try to link one common topic to several comments that do not seem to go together well at all. For example, you could be asked to write according to the following formula:

$$A \longrightarrow B$$
$$B \longrightarrow C$$

You could write an incoherent pair of sentences to fit this formula by producing *Michelle had to buy a new pen. The pen that the President used to sign that bill is in the Smithsonian Museum.*

1. $A \longrightarrow B$
   $B \longrightarrow C$
   $C \longrightarrow D$
   $D \longrightarrow E$

2. $A \longrightarrow B \ (=B1 + B2)$
   $B1 \longrightarrow C$
   $B2 \longrightarrow D$

3. $A \longrightarrow B$
   $A \longrightarrow C$
   $A \longrightarrow D$

4. $A \ (=A1 + A2) \longrightarrow B$
   $A1 \longrightarrow C$
   $A2 \longrightarrow D$

5. $A \longrightarrow B$
   $B \longrightarrow C$
   $A \longrightarrow D$
   $D \longrightarrow E$

TOPICAL STRUCTURE ANALYSIS

There is an easy and helpful method to analyze whether you are creating a coherent set of topics in essays. Start with a regular sheet of lined writing paper. Then add some vertical lines to it so that you end up with rows and columns of boxes. Finally, number the rows from top to bottom along the left side of the paper, and number the columns from left to right along the top of the paper. The numbers along the left will indicate how many topics are in the essay being analyzed. And the numbers along the top will give an indication of the topical diversity in the essay; the higher the number, the greater the topical diversity. When you are finished, your sheet should look something like this:

	1	2	3	4	5	6	7
1							
2							
3							
4							
5							
6							
7							

Now go through the paragraph or essay that you wish to analyze and underline the topics of all the independent clauses. Working with independent clauses is sufficient for our purposes, unless they express metadiscourse. Write the first topic in the upper left corner, in the box where row 1 and column 1 intersect.

Now look at the second topic. If it is identical or closely related to the first topic, write it in the box formed where row 2 intersects column 1. If it is different from the first topic, write it in the box where row 2 intersects column 2. At the same time, if the second topic is not closely related to any of the material in the first sentence (topic or comment), put an asterisk by it.

Now move to the third topic. There are several possible responses to it. If it is identical to topic 1, put it in the box where row 3 intersects column 1. If it is identical to topic 2, and both of them are different from topic 1, put topic 3 immediately below topic 2, in the box formed where row 3 intersects column 2. If topic 3 is different from topic 2, which is also different from topic 1, put topic 3 in the box formed by the intersection of row 3 and column 3. If topic 3 is also unrelated to any of the material in sentences 1 and 2 (topics and comments), put an asterisk by it.

The general principle underlying this method of analysis is that one topic is listed directly below any other that it is identical or closely related to. If it is different from all preceding topics, it will be listed one column to the right of the prior topic. Finally, if a topic is unrelated to any of the information in earlier topics and comments, it should have an asterisk by it.

If most of the topics for an essay are listed to the left of a topical structure analysis chart, and if few of them have an asterisk by them, you have a good indication that the essay develops a coherent set of topics and is probably coherent itself.

However, if the topics move off far to the right of a chart (that is, if the essay has a high degree of topical diversity), and if some of them have an asterisk, you have a good indication that the essay develops an incoherent set of topics and is probably less than fully coherent itself.

In the studies that have been done in this area, researchers have found that essays which get poor grades from trained evaluators generally have little elaboration on each of several topics. If they do elaborate on a topic, they do so to excess, moving into more and more minute details and ignoring the other general topics. Writers of such essays seem to work in a scatter-shot manner; they seem to develop essays by means of free association.

On the other hand, essays that receive high grades from evaluators have quite a bit and almost equal amounts of elaboration on each of fewer topics. This is especially the case early in essays, at the more general levels. Writers of such essays show that they have a unifying intention governing their essays.

We should look at how topical structure analysis is applied to a paragraph or two. I will start with the following:

> There are people, however, who know their own minds perfectly well and who approach the purchase of a funeral much as they would any other transaction. They are, by the nature of things, very much in the minority. Most frequently they are not in the immediate family of the deceased but are friends or representatives of the family. Their experiences are interesting because to some extent they throw into relief the irrational quality of the funeral transaction.
>
> (Jessica Mitford, *The American Way of Death*, p. 27)

First, we should identify the topics. I will pull them out as follows:

people
They
they
Their experiences

Now we can fill these in on a topical structure analysis chart:

		1	2	3	4
1	people				
2	They				
3	they				
4	Their experiences				

People, *They*, and *they* are in the same column, since they all refer to the same entities. *Their experiences* is also in that column, since it refers to things that are closely related to these people.

As you can see, all the topics are to the left. None has an asterisk by it. Such a diagram would lead us to say that this is a very coherent set of topics and probably a coherent paragraph. And I trust that most people would in fact find this a coherent paragraph.

Now consider the end of one of the student paragraphs from Chapter One. I use only the end of the paragraph, since it is long enough to make my point and since it is the part of the paragraph that seems to be most incoherent:

> Strong external constraints characterize the low suicide areas. The high suicide areas are characterized by weak external constraints. Anomie is common to areas with high suicide rates. This is when people are in a severe state of confusion. Anomic suicide usually results from temporary but abrupt alteration in the norms of society. First, sudden social changes, such as the Great Depression, seemed to be associated with high suicide rates. Second, Durkheim feels that any disturbance in the everyday pattern can lead to an increased suicide rate.

Again, the first step is to identify the topics. I will pull them out as follows:

Strong external constraints
The high suicide areas
Anomie
This
Anomic suicide
sudden social changes, such as the Great Depression
any disturbance in the everyday pattern

Now we can fill in the topical structure analysis chart:

	1	2	3	4
1	Strong external constraints			
2		The high suicide areas		
3			Anomie*	
4			This	
5			Anomic suicide	
6				sudden social changes, such as the Great Depression
7				any disturbance in the everyday pattern

   This partial paragraph is not the most incoherent piece of prose one could find, but it is a good example, since it is not vastly different from much of the prose that many writers produce and since it shows many tendencies characteristic of incoherent prose: topics that move off to the right of the chart, one or more topics with an asterisk, and very little development of any topic. Moreover, the last sentence makes reading more difficult because of the metadiscourse ("Durkheim feels") that appears where we expect to find the topic.
   One important characteristic of incoherent prose that topical structure analysis does not reveal immediately is the semantic

distance between one topic and another that might not be far to the right of it on the chart. For instance, in the other student paragraph that I used in Chapter One, the first sentence is, "Popular music is beneficial to society because it can be used to bring a positive message to people." The fifth sentence is, "Because certain persons have used nuclear energy for killing and destruction does not mean that nuclear energy is essentially bad."

The paragraph that these sentences appear in is short, and some of the topics in it are closely related to the first topic. Therefore, the topic of the fifth sentence will not appear many columns to the right of the topic of the first sentence. And that might lead us to think that the paragraph is in fact quite coherent. But we have to look at the semantic distance between topics one and five. That distance verges on the incredible: from popular music to using nuclear energy for killing and destruction. We might well wonder how someone could possibly move such a distance in only a few sentences. More to the point, we might wonder what kind of purpose could justify such a move. I can imagine such purposes, but they all go beyond making a claim about the benefits of popular music.

In this light, it is clear that we should not use topical structure analysis to give us only a structural image for a paragraph or essay that we can compare with the images for other paragraphs or essays. Of course, as we fill in the chart and move from one topic to the next, we must consider how similar in meaning the two topics are. But we must go beyond that and also consider how more widely separated topics compare in meaning.

If you bear all these things in mind, I trust that you will find topical structure analysis valuable in indicating how well your essays hang together. Most of the students with whom I have worked find it easy to do, quite interesting, and helpful. At a glance, they get a good indication of how connected their prose is. And with closer examination, they start to see precisely how they have linked one sentence to the next one and to more remote ones. They can chart how they have moved through an essay and decide whether they like that pathway. For these reasons, at some time after a first draft but before the day on which they submit final material, many of them find it worthwhile to do topical structure analysis. Then they can revise the topical structure if they deem it necessary.

One final implication of this sort of analysis that students usually pick up is that if they are blocked at points in their essays, they might be well served to go back to topics they wrote about earlier to see if they can and should develop them more. Many students find that they have not developed topics at general stages of their essays as much as readers might expect. At the same time, they might find that topics they have already written about can stimulate ideas about new topics.

Exercise Five

Working with the topics of all independent clauses, fill out a topical structure analysis chart for each of the following paragraphs. Then tell how coherent you think each paragraph is.

1. Burke invites his readers to search for cues to his motives. He so often repeats key-terms throughout the text—"clusters," "discontinuities," and "bridges"—that the reader turns them back on the text at hand. In his note to the introduction of the second edition, Burke acknowledges a reader's criticism, granting that his footnotes are a "blemish," but he leaves, even adds to them, explaining that they are the only way to trace the "radiating" material. The framing footnotes also provide discontinuities and perspectives by incongruity, gaps through which the reader can see to the intended, not merely the stated, meaning, if he is so inclined. Burke even accommodates his reader to his intended meaning by describing what has been omitted from the text (237). In *Attitudes Toward History*, Burke also begins to formulate his theory of identification, in which readers project themselves into the text, to share vicariously in the artistic experience and thereby to recognize the author's intention. In his afterword to the second edition, he provides one final frame of acceptance to his text by affirming his model of communication, "the most generalized statement of the principle of 'love'" (347).

   (Tilly Warnock, "Reading Kenneth Burke: Ways In, Ways Out, Ways Roundabout," *College English*, 48, January, 1986, p. 68)
   /

2. The natural properties of any medium permit it to imitate relatively few things directly, and a great many more signally. Imitation by signs may employ natural or artificial signs. These latter depend not upon the natural properties of the medium but upon convention. For example, in Noh drama, the hand passed before the mask indicates weeping; this is

an artificial sign of grief; it is possible only through convention, and can be understood only by those who know the convention.

(Elder Olson, *The Theory of Comedy*, p. 33)

3. Human beings are symbol-making creatures. Like Dr. Frankenstein, however, whose supercharged creation did a bit of unscheduled meandering and mayhem, we are often victimized by our unthinking, knee-jerk responses to symbols of our own invention. This automatic, unreflective, and usually inappropriate response to symbols is called a *signal reaction*. Pledges, oaths, slogans, ritualized greetings, chants, and buzz words in politics and advertising are a few examples of signal reactions at work. What is called for in each of these instances is not careful analysis and inquiry but rather a hair-trigger response, a Pavlovian conditioned reaction to a verbal stimulus.

(J. Dan Rothwell, *Telling It Like It Isn't*, p. 3)

4. The most prominent feature of the judicial opinion is that it is not an isolated exercise of power but part of a continuing and collective process of conversation and judgment. The conversation of which it is a part is not a political conversation of the usual sort, proceeding as such conversations ordinarily do—by a kind of jostling and compromise, focusing mainly on the problem of the immediate present—but a highly formal one, in which authoritative conclusions are reached after explicit argument. These decisions in their turn become the material of future arguments leading to future decisions, and so on in a continuing process of opening and closure, argument and judgment, of which no one can claim to foresee the end.

(James Boyd White, *When Words Lose Their Meanings*, p. 264)

5. Johanson and White argue that the Afar specimens and Mary Leakey's Laetoli fossils are identical in form and belong to the same species. They also point out that the Afar and Laetoli bones and teeth represent everything we know about hominids exceeding 2.5 million years in age—all the other African specimens are younger. Finally, they claim that the teeth and skull pieces of these old remains share a set of features absent in later fossils and reminiscent of apes. Thus, they assign the Laetoli and Afar remains to a new species, *A. afarensis*.

(Stephen Jay Gould, "Our Greatest Evolutionary Step," *The Panda's Thumb*, p. 126.)

Exercise Six

The topical coherence of each of the following paragraphs can be improved. Revise each to keep most, if not all, of the information and to achieve a more coherent topical structure.

1. A liberal arts education is valuable for all those entering college today. A firm sense of history and a perspective on cultural changes are given to people by it. Moreover, students are introduced to the best writers in several traditions by it. Finally, and most important, the ability to think critically is fostered by it. This ability is essential in order for a democratic society to endure.

2. The Granite Park Chalet was found by them after an all-day scramble up rockslides. Shelter, several cots, and facilities for preparing meals were provided by the chalet. But roasted nuts and lemon drops were their meals. The safari store had had these items on sale.

3. Turkey Run, Brown County, and Pokagon are the McKenzies' favorite state parks in Indiana. The canyons and crevices are the best features of Turkey Run. Turkey Run also has both modern and primitive campgrounds. The scenic overlooks, especially in the autumn, are the outstanding features of Brown County. The McKenzies drive all the roads and stop at the overlooks for pictures. And the many facilities for winter recreation are the most attractive features of Pokagon. These facilities attract people from all over the upper Midwest.

4. Although the baseball team had a poor record this year, there were several bright spots in its season. The fielding of several of the first-year players was the first bright spot. The second was the smart base-running by some of the players. The promise shown by two of the younger pitchers was the third bright spot. Finally, the fourth bright spot was the positive attitude that the team displayed, even in adversity. This attitude should provide a strong foundation for progress for the team in the future.

5. The two researchers primarily responsible for those developments were Watteau and Valence. The configurations of the fifth dimension were laid out with exquisite precision by Watteau. And Valence showed how to harness the energy of atoms that are superheated while captured in a magnetic field.

TO REVIEW:
TOPICAL COHERENCE

This chapter develops ideas that we touched on in Chapter Three, where we considered how to select appropriate topics for sentences. I noted there that one important way to decide what to focus on in a sentence is to keep in mind what you have focused on in preceding sentences. That advice is based on a functional view of coherence that is developed here: Writers help readers move through their essays if they give them a coherent set of topics to focus on.

The topical progressions described in this chapter are means to use to work toward coherent sets of topics. And topical structure analysis can help chart how coherent sets of topics actually are. Above all, though, we must keep in mind that even if sentences are linked through the repetition of words, they do not necessarily form a coherent passage unless the writer controls them in accordance with an overall intention in order to fulfill purposes in actual situations.

FURTHER READING

Connor, U. (1984). "A Study of Cohesion and Coherence in English as a Second Language Students' Writing," *Papers in Linguistics, 17,* 301-316.

Daneš, F. (1974). "Functional Sentence Perspective and the Organization of the Text." In F. Daneš (Ed.), *Papers on Functional Sentence Perspective* (pp. 106-128). The Hague: Mouton.

Dillon, G. L. (1981). *Constructing Texts, Elements of a Theory of Composition and Style.* Bloomington: Indiana University Press.

Enkvist, N. E. (1973). "Theme Dynamics and Style: An Experiment." *Studia Anglica Posnaniensia, 5,* 127-135.

Glatt, B. S. (1982). "Defining Thematic Progressions and Their Relationship to Reader Comprehension." In M. Nystrand (Ed.), *What Writers Know: The Language, Process, and Structure of Written Discourse* (pp. 87-103). New York: Academic Press.

Reinhart, T. (1980). "Conditions for Text Coherence." *Poetics Today, 1,* 161-180.

Scinto, L. F. M. (1983). "Functional Connectivity and the Communicative Structure of Text." In J. S. Petöfi & E. Sözer (Eds.), *Micro and Macro Connexity of Texts* (pp. 23-115). Hamburg: Buske Verlag.

Witte, S. P. (1983). "Topical Structure and Revision: An Exploratory Study." *College Composition and Communication, 34,* 313-341.

Using Sets of Sentence Topics Appropriate to Overall Methods of Development

An utterance has meaning only in the entire context and through our knowledge of the world.
—Irena Bellert, "On a Condition of the Coherence of Texts"

Step 2 in my argument is that thematic content correlates with the method of development of a text and with the nature of that text.
—Peter H. Fries, "On the Status of Theme in English: Arguments from Discourse"

In Chapter Seven, I stressed that in portions of essays or in entire essays you should strive to make your sets of sentence topics coherent. That is, topics in such sets should be identical, closely related, or derivable from material preceding them.

But I wrote very little about what exactly those topics should be. And much needs to be written, because writers who mechanically follow the fifth guideline could make their topics go well together as a set without paying enough attention to what information those topics convey.

THE SIXTH GUIDELINE

Therefore, I now move to a sixth guideline for clear and coherent prose. In general, express in your sets of sentence topics material that is consistent with your overall method of development for an essay.

With this guideline, I assume several things. First, I assume that skilled writers think very carefully about the rhetorical situations they participate in. In other words, they consider what it is that they are essentially trying to do with a piece of writing, what context they are writing in, who their readers are, what their readers already know about their subject matter, and what their readers expect to learn. As the writers analyze such matters, they decide upon or discover an overall method of development for their essays. They decide how to proceed in conveying information to readers and in discussing it with them.

For instance, in a piece of writing in which someone decides to describe an abandoned cabin to readers who have never seen it, she might proceed by telling a story of how she discovered the cabin, explored it, and reacted to it. The focus would be on her, the teller of the tale. Or she might choose a different method of development, that of providing a kind of guidebook tour of the cabin, with the readers imaginatively taking the tour. Here the focus would be on the readers moving along on the tour. Or the writer might decide to develop an essay by focusing on aspects of the cabin without worrying very much about how those aspects relate to each other in space. Here the focus would be on the various aspects. And there are other ways to develop such an essay, as well as many ways to combine methods of development.

In any case, I assume further that whatever method of development writers select, that method will be closely related to what they focus on in sentences. Thus their method of development will largely reveal itself in topics, the focal points for sentences. In other words, in effective, coherent prose, the sentence topics will usually be consistent with a method of development that is appropriate for the writer's overall purpose and meets readers' expectations well.

Having written this, I must add that I cannot provide a neat chart showing how certain subject matters lend themselves to certain purposes in writing, which lend themselves to certain methods of development, which in turn lend themselves to certain kinds of sentence topics, In all of these areas there are simply too many variables and relationships.

What I hope to do is to make you more sensitive to these variables and relationships and more skilled in working with them as you go through the writing process. I hope you will think more about different possible purposes you might have in writing about essen-tially the same subject matter. I hope that you will explore the methods of development you could employ and that you are able to justify the one or the combination you ultimately choose. Finally, I hope that you carefully consider how various methods of develop-ment will manifest themselves in sentence topics and that your method of development corresponds well to your topics.

What should become clear here is a point closely related to one I made in Chapter Two. There I indicated that there is not one and only one way to construct a sentence about something in the world. There are several possibilities, depending on what you wish to focus on and what you wish to convey about it. Moreover, what you wish to focus on and what you wish to convey about it are dependent on some greater purpose for writing the sentence at all.

Reality does not force us to write about it in only one way. It does not present itself to us with a ready-made sentence form attached. We take different perspectives on reality, and we use sentences to reflect those perspectives. In so doing, we build up an overall view of the world for ourselves. And often we try to communicate our view to others and to interact with them about that view. You may find my claim somewhat extreme, but I would say that with most sentences we use (one exception being those sentences in which we interact socially with no intention of giving or receiving information: "How are you doing?"), we are trying to communicate to others a view of reality.

What I claim about sentences I would also claim about sets of sentences. An essay about an abandoned cabin need not appear in one and only one form. Thinking about readers' needs and expectations, a writer can formulate different overall purposes that lead him or her to develop essays in different ways. And these different ways correlate with different kinds of material in topics.

To encapsulate much of this discussion: The sentence topics in a well-written essay should provide good clues to the way in which the writer has chosen to develop it. That method of development is not the only one possible; it is one of several, the one or the combination that best suits the writer's purpose. Therefore, just as a sentence topic can reveal what perspective on things the writer is taking in that sentence, so the set or sets of sentence topics can reveal what perspective on things the writer is taking in the essay.

SENTENCE TOPICS AND
METHODS OF DEVELOPMENT

An example or two should make the preceding discussion clearer. Imagine that I am asked to write a very short piece on the sound system of language. My purpose is basically informative, since I am asked to shed some light on this subject for those who have heard about elements of the system (in particular the phone-types, which are all possible sounds in a language; and the phonemes, which are the sounds that signal distinctions in meaning) but are just beginning to learn details about these elements.

I immediately face several choices, most particularly about how to develop the piece. After I think about the situation for a while, I decide to develop it by focusing on the phonemes, since they are the significant sounds of language and the key, I believe, to relating sounds and sense in language. Thus I decide to inform readers about the sound system by focusing on phonemes.

Then I produce the following draft:

Phonemes, important elements of the sound system of language, are called the significant sounds of language. Phonemes are usually groups or sets of phone-types. A phoneme may be constituted by only one phone-type. For example, the /š/ phoneme is made up of only one phone-type, the [š]. More often, though, a phoneme is constituted by two or more phone-types. For instance, the /f/ phoneme is made up of two phone-types, the [f] and the [Φ]. Thus the phonemes in a language are not as numerous as the phone-types.

To illustrate my major point here, I should pull the topics out of this paragraph and list them:

Phonemes, important elements of the sound system of language

Phonemes

A phoneme

the /š/ phoneme

a phoneme

the /f/ phoneme

the phonemes in a language

This list shows that the set of topics in this paragraph is very coherent. But it also shows how consistently I followed through on my projected method of development. I had decided to develop this paragraph by focusing on the phoneme. And a reference to a phoneme or to phonemes appears in each topic. This paragraph, therefore, conforms well to the sixth guideline. Its topics are consistent with its overall method of development.

But is this paragraph the only possible response to my original assignment? Not at all. Keeping the same purpose as that which motivated the first paragraph, I could decide that those who are learning details about elements of the sound system of language should concentrate on phone-types. I could therefore decide to develop my paragraph by focusing on phone-types. This paragraph could convey almost all of the information that the first paragraph does, but it would do so from a different perspective.

A draft of the second paragraph looks like this:

Phone-types, important elements of the sound system of language, are called the building blocks of language. Phone-types usually occur in groups or sets known as phonemes. One phone-type may constitute a phoneme. For example, the [š] phone-type by itself makes up the /š/ phoneme. More often, though, two or more phone-types constitute a phoneme. For instance, the two phone-types [f] and [Φ] constitute the /f/ phoneme. Thus the phone-types in a language are more numerous than the phonemes.

This paragraph addresses the same general issue as the first one, and it conveys essentially the same information. But it does so from a different perspective. It focuses on phone-types, whereas the first focuses on phonemes.

Listing the topics in this paragraph makes this clear:

Phone-types, important elements of the sound system of language
Phone-types
One phone-type
the [š] phone-type by itself
two or more phone-types
the two phone-types [f] and [Φ]
the phone-types in a language

The list shows that this paragraph too follows the sixth guideline well. All of the topics name phone-types or a particular phone-type or two, and my method of development was to focus on phone-types.

Now reflect a little on these two paragraphs. They are about equally long, they contain only grammatical sentences, they convey essentially the same bits of information, the sets of topics in both are coherent, and each set of topics is consistent with a particular method of development. Is one paragraph better than the other? As I wrote in my discussion of the use of metadiscourse in Chapter 4, again I must write that the answer depends on several things, only a few of which I can address here.

Both paragraphs work toward fulfilling the basic purpose of informing readers about details of the sound system of language. According to this criterion, we cannot really say that one paragraph is better than the other. But much of the answer would depend on my readers, for, although both paragraphs present essentially the same kernels of information, they do so from different perspectives. And one of these perspectives may be clearer to certain readers than the other. Certainly one perspective would lead readers to structure information in their memories differently from the way that the other perspective does. Readers would probably say these paragraphs are actually about different specific subjects.

For readers who know a little more about the sound system and would perhaps learn best by focusing on the elements that have the most direct connection to other systems (for example, the system of meaning), the first paragraph is probably better because it focuses on the links between sound and meaning, the phonemes. But for those who know somewhat less about the sound system and would probably learn best by focusing on what is close to the foundation of the sound system, the second paragraph would probably be better because it focuses on the phone-types, which many linguistics texts take as the starting point in the study of sounds.

Making such decisions is difficult. Sometimes it is nearly impossible. For example, it is most difficult when you have no idea or only a slight idea of who your readers will be. But you should at least pose such problems for yourself as you plan your writing. In my experience, when students begin to wrestle with such problems, they usually come up with solutions. And when I ask them to justify their proposed solutions, they usually do a good job of it. To my mind, the key is learning to think first about specific aspects of purpose, context, audience, methods of development, and sets of sentence topics.

Exercise One

Below are several words or phrases that name subjects for possible essays. For each, list several different perspectives that could be taken on it. Compare your responses with those of others. For example, you could be asked to write about choosing a major in college. You could focus on things such as the interest of the major to you, the job possibilities the major opens up, or the skills the major develops, among other possibilities.

1. Life in a fraternity or sorority
2. Professional football
3. Acid rain
4. Insecticides
5. Terrorism
6. A fulfilling career
7. National parks in the United States
8. Programs for teacher education

9. Unemployment
10. The welfare system

Exercise Two

Each of the following short passages focuses on an object, event, or action from a certain perspective. Tell what perspective each passage reveals, rewrite each to focus on something different yet still appropriate, and then discuss briefly in what situation each version might be the preferable one. For example, a passage could treat the subject of crime in large cities by focusing on the role of the police in preventing crime. Such a focus would be appropriate for readers concerned with law enforcement. The passage could be rewritten to focus on what motivates people to commit crimes. Such a focus would be appropriate for readers concerned with social deviance.

1. When teachers discover that some of their students have cheated on examinations, they face a trying situation. In the first place, they have to establish beyond doubt that the students did indeed cheat. Often they present students with hard evidence of cheating only to receive firm denials of wrongdoing. Second, they often feel obligated to discover the students' motives for cheating. Doing this can be difficult, for most teachers are used to treating students as if they always behaved ethically, and they are unaccustomed to discovering—as a detective or psychologist might—why some students do the dishonest things they do. Finally, teachers face the decision of how to punish students who cheat. They know that to be fair to the honest students, they must punish the dishonest ones. But many find their options limited or distasteful.

2. Managing a large wilderness preserve such as Glacier National Park is a monumentally difficult task. The park rangers feel pressures from all sides. On one hand, they hear from supporters of pristine wilderness areas that they should open fewer campgrounds and carve fewer trails out of the sides of mountains. On the other hand, they feel pressure from those who enjoy the mountains but do not wish to backpack in order to stay in them and explore them. The most notable issue they confront is how to manage the grizzlies. Many rangers believe that the grizzlies deserve to stay in the park, where they have always lived. They maintain that the grizzlies are integrally associated with the wilderness atmosphere that pervades the park. At the same time, however, most

rangers fear the occasional confrontations between grizzlies and humans. They warn people to take precautions, and they often close dangerous trails. But with so many people and grizzlies in the same limited area, some confrontations each year are inevitable. All such problems will probably remain with the rangers as long as we have the park as we know it.

3. For student teachers, the first day in front of a class can be terrifying. They are usually observers in classrooms before they have to teach. But observing is far different from teaching. Once they face the class on their own, they usually worry about many things. They worry about whether the students will obey them, be quiet, and give them a chance to start their lessons. Further, they worry that if they have to punish students, the students will not accept the punishment but will work to undermine all of their authority. Usually, however, student teachers get students to come to order and manage to start their lessons. But then they worry about whether they have prepared interesting material. What they think is interesting may not be interesting at all for their students. And even when they succeed in sparking their students' interest and curiosity, they worry about whether they have prepared enough material. Perhaps nothing is as frightening to them as finishing a lesson fifteen minutes early and having nothing else prepared for their students to do.

4. Today's writing teachers stress many things that those in the past usually paid little attention to. Today teachers try to help their students develop an approach to the processes of writing that they will be able to use after the course, in many situations and for many purposes. Thus teachers try to help students learn specific techniques that will enable them to think of material to write about. These invention techniques should be useful throughout the students' writing careers. Teachers today also stress that there are many ways in which a paragraph can be developed and that students should select the way that best fits their purpose and situation. Finally, teachers work hard to get their students to see that revision should be "reseeing" or "reconceptualization." It should involve more than a mere tidying-up of an essay. Teachers are most pleased when they find that their students not only write well in class but also develop a procedure for writing well long after the course is finished.

5. Although most teenage girls complain about the difficulties associated with dating, the dating process is really much more trying for boys. In the first place, they face the trauma of making the first call, a call that is difficult enough in itself. But it is all the more difficult for those boys in

households with only one phone, which is usually located precisely where at least three other members of the family can listen in and contribute choice comments. Second, the boys face the pressure of deciding what to do. Usually they can come up with ideas for five or six different dates. But after that, many of them would like some help discovering things to do. If they ask their dates, however, they usually receive only an "I don't care" in response. Finally, the boys are subjected to nearly unbearable pressure from their peers. They are told whom to ask out, whom not to ask out, where to go, where not to go, what to wear, what not to wear, and countless other things. It is a wonder that they survive the ordeal.

SENTENCE TOPICS AND METHODS OF DEVELOPMENT, CONTINUED

So far I have discussed methods of development as ways to focus on different aspects of something. We can extend the discussion by seeing that some methods of development involve taking different approaches to the very same thing or situation. Still, however, such methods reflect themselves in sets of sentence topics. In other words, the way you decide to focus your entire essay should affect what you decide to focus on in individual sentences.

Again, some examples should make this clearer. Suppose you are asked to write a primarily descriptive paper about some building that has affected you emotionally. You can assume that your readers have not seen the building. After some thought, you decide to write about the abandoned cabin you discovered as a youngster while on vacation with your family.

You could develop the essay in many different ways. You could make it a kind of narrative, a story of how you first discovered the cabin and how it affected you. If you chose such a method of development, you would probably focus on the actor in the narrative, since stories usually center on actors. Therefore, many sentences would focus on you, and the piece as a whole would focus on you, the actor in the story.

Such a piece could appear as follows:

I discovered the abandoned cabin when I was eight. I was vacationing with my family on the shores of Whitefish Bay at the time, and one afternoon I wandered off through timothy fields toward Dollar Settlement to pick raspberries. I found some excellent patches of berries and quickly lost track of where I had been. Soon, though, I stepped on a weathered piece of siding and jumped back in surprise. When I looked up, I saw what seemed to be a homesteader's cottage slowly being absorbed into the land.

Even though I could hear my parents saying that I should stay out of places like this, I decided that I had to investigate. I started by trying the paintless back door. It was nailed shut. But then I noticed that a nearby lower window had lost its panes of glass, and I carefully stuck my head through it. It opened into a shallow, dank basement. In it, I saw several Mason jars, some still holding what looked like mashed yams. Near them I saw a crosscut saw and a set of 1932 Michigan license plates. I backed away as curiosity swept over me. Who had canned the yams? Who had used the saw? Who had saved the old license plates? But then I felt a great sense of loss. Look at what their efforts had come to.

If you go back over this short piece, you will find that most of the sentence topics are *I*. *I* refers to the only actor in this short sketch, the one who pushes the story from one event to the next and who ends up feeling curiosity and a sense of loss. Such sentence topics correspond well with a method of development for a personal narrative.

But there are other ways to develop the same material in response to the same assignment. You could write something like a guidebook description of how to discover the abandoned cabin, indicating to your readers how to find it, what to look for in it, and how to expect to react to it. It would be natural to focus on your readers in the topics of such a piece, since they, you assume, will be following your directions in their imaginations.

Such a piece could look like this:

You will find the abandoned cabin on the shores of Whitefish Bay, just a little east of Dollar Settlement. You will discover it most easily if you take Forest Highway 13 to Dollar Settlement, turn to the east on Lakeshore Drive, and go another 1.6 miles. After you've parked your car off the road, you should head across the timothy fields toward the lake. You will have to work your way through some thick raspberry patches, and you should watch for an especially thick patch with a birch tree on its western edge.

It is that patch that guards the cabin. You should approach the cabin from the back, taking care not to puncture your boots on the rusty nails in scattered pieces of siding on the ground. You will find the back door nailed shut, so to get a view inside, try the nearby lower window that has lost its panes of glass. When you poke your head through the window, you will be looking directly into a shallow, dank basement. In it you will see several Mason jars, some still holding what looks like mashed yams. Near them you will see a rusty crosscut saw and a set of 1932 Michigan license plates. You may wonder who had once lived here and who had canned the yams, used the saw, and saved the old plates. And if you dwell on these thoughts, you may feel a great sense of loss over what their efforts had come to.

In this piece, nearly all the topics are *You*. Thus, here again, what appears in the topics is consistent with the overall method of development because the *you* refers to readers who would actually or imaginatively follow the directions that appear in the essay. And the original plan was to take a guidebook-like approach with the readers as the focal point.

But even this method of development does not exhaust the possibilities for responses to this assignment. You could choose to develop it by focusing on parts of the abandoned cabin and some of their spatial relationships and then by moving to statements of what emotions seeing the parts might cause. In such a case, references to aspects of the cabin will appear in most of the sentence topics.

Such an essay might look like this:

The abandoned cabin stands on the shores of Whitefish Bay, just east of Dollar Settlement. It stands in a meadow where someone had once cultivated timothy and where now the raspberries are increasing their territory, patch extending into patch.

The cabin sits directly in front of one of the larger raspberry patches. Its roof is pockmarked, many of the shingles having been blown off in November storms. The four walls stand at various angles, and the ground seems to be sucking them in, a little more each season. There is only one door, the one in the back, and it is nailed shut. But there are several windows, one of which—the lower one near the door—has lost all of its panes of glass. That window opens into a shallow, dank basement. The basement still holds several Mason jars, some containing what looks like mashed yams. Near them lie a rusty crosscut saw and some 1932 Michigan license plates. The cabin itself, and especially the objects in its basement, stir questions: Who had canned the yams? used the saw? saved the license plates? They can also lead viewers to feel a sense of loss over what the people's efforts had come to.

Most of the topics here are consistent with the method of development for this piece. Most of them include references to the cabin itself or to parts of it. And the method of development involves focusing on parts of the cabin. This particular method of development is probably the one that most people associate with descriptive writing.

These three methods of development are not the only ways to structure an essay about the abandoned cabin. We could focus more on the spatial relationships among its parts, we could focus on the step-by-step process of its disintegration, we could focus on more artifacts as clues to its builder and former inhabitants, or we could focus on the many sounds that the dilapidated structure makes.

And there would be this many or more possible methods of development for other assignments—focusing on steps in a procedure, or steps in a process, or a problem and its possible solutions, to name just a few. Moreover, one essay may employ more than one method of development, moving from one method in one section to another and yet another. Or perhaps an essay will combine two or more simple methods of development in the same section. Finally, several different sets of sentence topics could probably be justified as consistent with the same method of development. It is clear, then, that we have pushed the matter of sentence topics into complex territory, which will need more exploration in the future.

To return to the three short essays I wrote, I would not claim that they are the best that could be written according to the three methods of development I chose. Still, they serve to make the point that here we have three essays on the same subject matter conveying much of the same information. What is most responsible for making them different? I would say it is their different methods of development and the different patterns of topicalization that these correlate with.

Which of these three essays is the best? It depends on the rhetorical situation. That is, it depends on the writer's purpose, the readers, and the overall context. One of these essays might fit a particular rhetorical situation better than the others. And a different one might fit a different rhetorical situation better than the others. Each seems to be written to fit a particular situation.

The writer of the first essay responds as if asked to tell what happened near a building and how he or she felt about it. It conveys a very personal message, and the emotions described seem immediate and genuine. But it does not give readers the clearest picture of the cabin.

The writer of the second essay responds as if asked to tell someone how to find the cabin, what especially to look for in it, and what emotions one can expect to feel in response to the sights. It draws the reader in immediately and thoroughly. But it demands readers who are willing to follow a guidebook.

The writer of the third piece responds as if asked to describe the salient aspects of the cabin and—to some degree—how they relate to each other in space. This piece probably comes closest to conveying a picture of the cabin and its setting. But the mention of emotions might strike some as tacked on and at odds with what earlier might seem close to objective description.

Each method of development has advantages and some probable disadvantages, and you could spend a good deal of time debating them. The key skill, though, is deciding in what situation the advantages of an essay would be highlighted and its disadvantages would seem unimportant. Thus, as you write, it is very important that you examine the rhetorical situation that you find yourself in: What are you being asked to do? to or for whom? why? in what context? Once you begin to answer such questions well, it should be easier to decide on an appropriate method of development and to see how that method should govern your choice of sentence topics.

Exercise Three

Use each one of the three methods of development that I used to write the pieces about the abandoned cabin near Dollar Settlement to produce three different short essays on the subject of a museum or some other building that you know quite well.

Exercise Four

In each of the following cases, I will provide you with two possible subject matters and a method of development. Use the method of development to structure a short piece on one of the subject matters.

1. **Subject matters:** a. leaving home for an extended period of time for the first time
   b. learning how to drive a car
   Method of development: a story, with the focus on you

2. **Subject matters:** a. a method of writing essays
                          b. a method of studying for examinations
    Method of development: a description and explanation of a procedure, with the focus on steps in the procedure

3. **Subject matters:** a. advice about selecting a topic for a long essay
                          b. advice about selecting a major in college
    Method of development: a description and explanation of a procedure, with the focus on your readers going through the steps of the procedure

4. **Subject matters:** a. your favorite hiking trail
                          b. the landscape you most despise
    Method of development: a description, with the focus on aspects

5. **Subject matters:** a. coping with friends who ask you to collaborate in schemes for cheating
                          b. managing your time
    Method of development: an explanation and exploration of a problem, with the focus on aspects of the problem and on possible solutions

TO REVIEW:
SETS OF SENTENCE TOPICS AND
METHODS OF DEVELOPMENT

Earlier we saw that sentences reveal what perspectives writers take on things. In this chapter we see that sets of sentence topics reveal what larger perspectives writers take on things. The sets of topics in an essay should be consistent with the overall method of development for that essay.

It is not possible to show all conceivable correspondences among subject matters, various methods of development, and different sets of sentence topics. Such work would extend into infinity. But it is possible for writers to become more skilled in analyzing their rhetorical situations. They can grow to understand better their subject matters, their tasks, their readers, and their contexts. And as they develop these skills, they will become better able to select appropriate methods of development and to relate these to appropriate sets of sentence topics. All of these activities are at the heart of rhetorical skill.

FURTHER READING

Bracewell, R. J., C. H. Frederiksen, and J. D. Frederiksen (1982). "Cognitive Processes in Composing and Comprehending Discourse," *Educational Psychologist, 17*, 146-164.

Enkvist, N. E. (1978). "Coherence, Pseudo-Coherence, and Non-Coherence." In J. O. Östman (Ed.), *Cohesion and Semantics* (pp. 109-128). Åbo Akademi: Publications of the Research Institute.

Fries, P. H. (1983). "On the Status of Theme in English: Arguments from Discourse." In J. S. Petöfi and E. Sözer (Eds.), *Micro and Macro Connexity of Texts* (pp. 116-149). Hamburg: Buske Verlag.

Kieras, D. E. (1981). "The Role of Major Referents and Sentence Topics in the Construction of Passage Macrostructure," *Discourse Processes, 4*, 1-15.

Witte, S. P. and R. D. Cherry (1986). "Writing Processes and Written Products in Composition Research." In C. R. Cooper and S. Greenbaum (Eds.), *Studying Writing: Linguistic Approaches* (pp. 112-153). Beverly Hills: Sage Publications.

Van Dijk, T. A. (1977). "Sentence Topic and Discourse Topic," *Papers in Slavic Philology, 1*, 49-61.

9

Identifying Given and New Information in Sentences

If what takes place lies entirely outside my expectations, so that nothing in my past experience provides the basis-for-modification, then I shall be able to make nothing of it: it might constitute "an experience" for somebody else, but for me it cannot.

> —James Britton, "Language and Experience," *Language and Learning*

. . . for the as yet unknown meaning would be incomprehensible were it not for the familiarity of the background it is set against.

> —Wolfgang Iser, *The Act of Reading*

Communication would be unnecessary if that which is to be communicated were not to some extent unfamiliar.

> —Wolfgang Iser, *The Act of Reading*

So, there is nothing new under the sun.

> —Ecclesiastes 1:9 (ASV)

In essence, novelty itself is rewarding.

> —Richard M. Restak, *The Brain: The Last Frontier*

After spending some time on the level of the full rhetorical situation with all of its complexities, I now move back to the level of the sentence to take a closer look at the nature of the information it conveys.

To prepare for this look, please examine the following clusters of sentences and try to tell what in general is wrong with or strange about all of them as judged by the standards of coherent prose:

1. Bruce had to start work very early on Tuesday. Samson is the name of a young dog. Last week Judy was on call at the hospital.
2. The President hailed the news that all the leading economic indicators in the United States had gone up. Mr. Reagan was most pleased to announce that the American economy was headed in a positive direction. Our country's chief of staff happily reported that the business climate in the United States was improving.
3. Tom is an avid fisherman. Bob also is an avid golfer.
4. Barb saw someone. It was Barb who saw James.
5. They are blue. In the closet are my running shoes.

It is quite easy to sense that there is something odd about each of these clusters. And it is relatively easy to describe what is odd about some of them. It is more difficult, however, to find a general way to explain what is strange about all of them. The earlier chapters of this book probably have led you to seek a general explanation in the nature of the topics and comments in these sentences. And scanning the topics and comments in these sentences will help you understand the flaw in some of these clusters quite well.

However, to get to the heart of the general problem, we have to consider some additional terms. Earlier I wrote of information that is probably familiar to readers, that is recoverable from earlier parts of an essay, that has been written about earlier in an essay. I also wrote about information that is probably unfamiliar to readers, that is not recoverable from earlier parts of an essay, that has not been written about earlier in an essay. Now I would like to introduce the terms *given information* and *new information* for these kinds of information.

And I will note that most sentences can be divided into two parts, one of which conveys given information, and the other of which conveys new information. This two-part division does not characterize all sentences, for occasionally sentences convey only given information, only new information, or information having different degrees of givenness and newness. But treating sentences as divisible into two parts will work best for our purposes here.

GIVEN INFORMATION

Given information in a sentence is that which readers know about from the rhetorical situation, which readers with even a minimal degree of knowledge about the world would know, which is mentioned prior to that sentence, or which is recoverable or inferable from material prior to that sentence.

If a sentence contains one of these kinds of given information, readers will be able to connect it to something they already know about. The given information provides them with a known starting point for a sentence, either in the situation, in what they know of the world, or in material expressed in earlier sentences.

Therefore, given information in sentences keeps readers from thinking they are reading a string of unrelated sentences. In simple terms, given information in a sentence ensures that that sentence will be connected to something readers already know about. Given information, then, is one of the chief means of bringing cohesiveness to an essay. To connect these points to some earlier ones, we can say that if an essay develops a coherent set of sentence topics, most of these topics will express given information. Most topics after the first either will have been expressed earlier or will be closely related to information conveyed earlier. Brief examples of different kinds of given information follow.

First, in most rhetorical situations, readers can take as given information the fact that an essay has an author. Thus, if the author were to refer to himself or herself with a pronoun (*I move now to my second argument*), readers would be able to understand to whom the *I* refers and would be able to treat it as given information. The same is true for direct references to the readers (*You will notice that . . .*) and to aspects of a problem that the essay is supposed to address. For instance, if a college president issued a written response to an attempted takeover of the administration building, she or he could refer to *the unfortunate incident that occurred yesterday*. Since this reference occurs in a situation in which all know who is writing to whom about what and for what purpose, the readers can treat this reference as given information.

Second, some things in the universe or some facts of life are unique and known to almost everyone. All readers with normal life experiences will treat these references as given information. In other words, references to some things are inherently given for all those who have not been isolated from the world or who can perceive the world normally. By way of example, references to things such as the sun and moon or to processes such as birth and death will be treated as given by readers.

Third, and most common, some information becomes given after it has been referred to once. Consider the following two sentences, the first of which functions to provide some context for the second:

> Bob lives in northern Michigan.
>
> He happens to enjoy cross-country skiing.

In the second sentence, *He* carries given information, since it refers to Bob, who is mentioned in the first sentence.

Finally, in the second sentence of the following pair, we treat some information as given since we can infer it from information in the first sentence:

> Last week Bob tried to make several gallons of maple syrup but had to settle for only two quarts.
>
> The sugar maples had run dry.

Even though the sugar maples are not mentioned in the first sentence, we can treat the reference to them in the second sentence as given. On the basis of what we know about natural maple syrup, we can infer that you cannot obtain and process it if the sugar maples have run dry.

Before we see the second sentence, we cannot predict with certainty that sugar maples will be mentioned. A sentence such as *All the firewood was wet* could have appeared. But once we see the sentence about the sugar maples, we do not treat it as unrelated to the first. We regard the two sentences as belonging together as a short text. The reference to the sugar maples allows us to connect the second sentence back to the first by means of an inference. Once we make this connection, we can interpret the second sentence as explaining why Bob was able to make only a little maple syrup.

As I noted above, information that becomes given through an inference is not completely predictable. But in some sentences with given information, if the given information were whited out, we would still be able to figure out what it is. For example, consider the following pair of sentences:

Wanda went to visit Audrey.

But _____ had already left for Pennsylvania.

In the second sentence, no one has trouble figuring out that *Audrey* or *she* would appear in the blank space. For this reason, especially in speech, many people simply delete given information. They are asked, "What does Meredy like to do?" and instead of saying "Meredy likes to swim," they respond by saying, "Swim." They leave out *Meredy likes to*, which in this context is all given information. Listeners know from the initial question that Meredy likes to do something.

Once we include a bit of information in an essay and it becomes given information when we refer to it again, it will usually appear in a different form on the second and subsequent occasions. To illustrate, at one point we could refer to Ronald Reagan. When we use this information again, we could write the words *Ronald Reagan* a second time. More likely, though, we would substitute other words. Most writing teachers would argue for varying the form of references to the same bit of given information, because doing so can help avoid monotonous repetitions.

For example, we could refer to Ronald Reagan with a long noun phrase (*The President of the United States of America*), with a synonym for that noun phrase (*The head of state in the U.S.A.*), with a reduced form of that noun phrase (*The President*), with a descriptive title (*That shrewd old actor*), with a pronoun (*He*), or even with no words at all if the given information happens to be obvious (*Ronald Reagan could have appointed Mr. Trauspiel to that post. Or he could have appointed Mrs. Kleinhoffen. But what did he finally do? Appointed a person of questionable ability.*).

Exercise One

Read each of the following pairs of sentences carefully, and then examine the second sentence in each pair to see if it contains some given information. If it does, tell what the information is, and indicate on what basis we treat it as given.

For example, consider the following two sentences:

The bus had to stop, since it had overheated.
The radiator had sprung a leak.

In the second sentence, we can treat *The radiator* as given information. We do so since a bus is referred to in the first sentence, and we can infer that buses have radiators; a radiator is part of a bus.

1. Roger bought a new heavy-duty truck.
   It should run for approximately ten years.
2. For all of these reasons their arguments are weak.
   I turn now to a summation.
3. Last night a car went off the road.
   The driver had apparently fallen asleep.
4. For the last two years Lisa has lived in Chicago.
   She works as a legal assistant.
5. Bud recently applied for a small loan.
   The banker was cordial and most easy to work with.
6. The night was perfect for fishing along the riverbank.
   The moon was very nearly full.
7. The shortstop threw his glove in disgust.
   The umpire had been out of position.
8. Houston received a very prestigious fellowship for graduate school.
   The composition handbooks are on the second shelf in the reserve reading room.
9. Jason cut his finger with a hunting knife.
   Blood seemed to be everywhere.
10. Wrigley Field is a wonderful place to take children.
    The fans rarely get into beer fights.

Exercise Two

In the second sentence of each of the following pairs is a blank. Tell what word or words writers would almost certainly use to fill the blank if they were using these sentences in a normal situation.

For example, consider the following two sentences:

Don was bitten by a small rattlesnake when he was ten miles away from camp.
_____ started to panic.

In this blank, writers would almost certainly insert *He*. *He* refers to Don, the only referent mentioned in the first sentence likely to start to panic.

1. Sharon stopped at Ned's office.
   But _____ was not in.
2. I went into the field and called for Mickey and his dog.
   The boy came, but _____ ran away.
3. What happened to your shoes?
   _____ were shredded by a pit bull.
4. Gary tried to call Anne on the phone.
   But the _____ was busy.
5. The umpire called the third strike.
   The _____ was out.
6. Lorraine told the twins to stay out of the water.
   The one obeyed, but the _____ walked right in.
7. A man called them as soon as they placed their advertisement.
   _____ wondered whether they had already sold their car.
8. A thunderstorm blew up just as they started to fish.
   The rain, wind, and _____ forced them off the lake.
9. Henry bragged to Ken about the contest.
   But _____ did not believe a word.
10. Howard ran at least fifteen miles on Saturday.
    His _____ were covered with blisters.

KINDS OF INFERENCES

Earlier I classified as given information an inference that a reader could make in one sentence on the basis of information in earlier sentences. There are some reasons to put such information in a category of its own. It is somewhat easier for readers to connect something mentioned in one sentence and that same thing mentioned in a later sentence than it is for them to connect one bit of information and another bit that can be inferred from it. The inference demands more mental work.

But I have chosen to classify inferences with the other kinds of given information because most inferences are not terribly difficult to make and because often information that is inferred from earlier sentences functions exactly as repeated information. Frequently what is inferred serves as the chief linkage between sentences. The inference allows readers to see the two sentences as connected, not as unrelated. Moreover, if we classify inferred information as given information, we can maintain a neat two-part classification of information: given and new information. And for the purposes of analyzing and improving one's own prose, this classification is probably the most useful.

When we infer one bit of information from another one, we do so on the basis of our knowledge of the world and relationships in it. A few of the relationships that we commonly recognize are explored below.

Usually we can infer the presence of unique objects known to all people (such as the sun and the moon) after only a brief description of a scene in which mention of such objects would be appropriate. Consider the following two sentences:

> The stars were clearly reflected in Croton Pond.
>
> The moon shone brightly and cast the birch trees into stark relief.

After reading the first sentence, we would have no trouble inferring that the moon was also visible. In fact, we might expect to hear of it, especially since the words *stars* and *moon* often occur near each other in passages. Therefore, in the second sentence, we treat *The moon* as given information; we view it as the link to the first sentence.

Second, after reading a reference to one object or event, we can infer the existence or occurrence of closely related objects and events. For instance, if we read *The pencils had all been sharpened recently*, we would have no difficulty inferring the presence of things such as paper, erasers, and paper clips. If the sentence about pencils were followed by *The paper was arranged in neat stacks*, we would be able to treat *The paper* as conveying given information.

Similarly, if we read a reference to a specific thing, we are able to infer the existence of the more general groups to which the specific thing belongs. If we read that *Tom had to bring a dog to the animal shelter*, we can infer the more general set to which the dog belongs (the set of animals). Thus, in a later sentence such as *The poor animal had cancer in his leg joints*, we would be able to realize that *dog* and *animal* refer to the same creature. In the later sentence, *The poor animal* functions as given information.

The reverse of this relationship sometimes allows us to make inferences. Having first read *The poor animal had cancer in his leg joints*, we are not necessarily able to predict that the animal is a dog. All dogs are animals, but not all animals are dogs. But once we read *The dog*, we will equate it with *The poor animal* unless the essay mentions other animals. And we will treat the reference to the dog as given information. We will use the reference to connect this sentence to the earlier one.

Another factor is that if we read about the whole of something, we can infer the existence of necessary, probable, or possible parts of it. If in one sentence we read about a room, we can infer that it necessarily has walls, probably has a window, and perhaps has a chandelier, with the easiest inferences associated with the necessary parts. We would be able to treat references to all these parts as given information when they appear in later sentences.

The reverse of this relationship also allows us to draw inferences. That is, if we read about a possible, probable, or necessary part of something, we are able to infer the existence of the whole of that thing. Reading that *The left elbow apparently has a bone chip in it* at one point, we would be able to infer the existence of a left arm and treat a later reference to it as given information.

Finally, if we read about causes of things, we should be able to infer the existence of necessary, probable, and possible effects, with the strongest inferences associated with the necessary effects. For instance, if we read that *He scratched his finger on a rusty nail*, we could see the scratch as the probable cause of infection. Therefore, if we next read the sentence *Infection spread into the base of his hand*, we would be able to treat the reference to infection as given information.

Or the other way around (going from effects to causes), if we read that *All the creeks are overflowing this morning*, we can infer that it rained or a dam burst or something happened to bring the levels of the creeks up. Thus, in a subsequent sentence such as *The rain lasted for seven hours*, we can treat *The rain* as conveying given information.

To sum up at this point, in most sentences in well-written prose, you should be able to find some given information. Given information is one of the main sources of cohesion in essays. It shows readers that they are reading about things they have read about already or about things that are closely related to things they have read about. It keeps readers from having to jump from one sentence to an unrelated one.

The given information is often that which all people normally know, which is obvious from the rhetorical situation, or which is mentioned earlier in an essay. Furthermore, sometimes something is mentioned in one sentence from which we can infer the existence of something that will be mentioned in a later sentence.

The connections between something mentioned and something else inferred from it are not as easily made as those between two references to the same thing. Inferences demand more mental effort. In many situations we can omit the second reference to the same thing (*Do you know what he did then? Just laughed*), but we usually cannot omit a reference to something we can infer. For example, we could not necessarily decipher all of *He scratched his finger on a rusty nail.* _____ *spread into the base of his hand.* Once we see the word *Infection*, however, we realize that it fits well within the framework of understanding that the sentence about scratching activates. And then we treat *Infection* as we would treat a repeated reference; we use it as the main linkage between these two sentences.

Exercise Three

Something in the second sentence of each of the following pairs of sentences can be inferred from information in the first sentence. In each case, tell what can be inferred and on the basis of what relationship it can be inferred. For example, consider the following two sentences:

He lay on the beach for only an hour but got a bad burn.
The sun had been very bright.

In the second sentence, we can infer the presence of the sun. We do so because we recognize it as the probable cause of the burn he got while lying on the beach.

1. Wanda took the picnic supplies out of the car.
   The plastic spoons had nearly melted.
2. He twisted his ankle trying to return a serve.
   The swelling took more than a week to go down.
3. This mower is on sale this week.
   The choke has several new features.
4. The wind howled around the cottage, forcing its way through cracks.
   The rain fell like a whip, lashing against the roof.
5. I had some misgivings about the transmission.
   But otherwise the car seemed to be in excellent condition.

6. The infection under his fingernail took nearly a month to clear up.
   The small cut on his finger had been more serious than anyone had thought.
7. The birds were calling lustily, busily laying claim to their territory.
   The sun had a rainbow around it, signaling a change in the weather.
8. His dog howled all night long.
   That crazy animal has a love affair with a full moon.
9. Daniel discovered an aluminum canoe in the bathhouse.
   Both paddles were cracked in half.
10. Yesterday they registered their daughter for preschool in the new private academy.
   The fee was surprisingly low.

Exercise Four

Use the sets of instructions below to create pairs of sentences, taking care to connect the second sentence to the first with the kind of inferable information specified.

For example, you could read the following: "Write two connected sentences. Make the topic of the second something that is a part of something mentioned in the first sentence." You could then write sentences such as these:

They tried to store all their climbing equipment in the trunk.

But the ice axe was too long.

1. Write two connected sentences. Make the topic of the second something closely related to something mentioned in the first.
2. Write two connected sentences. Make the topic of the second a specific manifestation of something more general mentioned in the first.
3. Write two connected sentences. Make the topic of the second a general term that includes something more specific mentioned in the first.
4. Write two connected sentences. Make the topic of the second a necessary part of something mentioned in the first.
5. Write two connected sentences. Make the topic of the second a possible part of something mentioned in the first.
6. Write two connected sentences. Make the topic of the second a whole that includes a part mentioned in the first.

7. Write two connected sentences. Make the topic of the second the cause of an effect mentioned in the first.
8. Write two connected sentences. Make the topic of the second an effect of a cause mentioned in the first.
9. Write two connected sentences. Make the topic of the second something closely associated with something mentioned in the first.
10. Write two connected sentences. Make the topic of the second something that is often written about when something in the first is written about.

NEW INFORMATION

By this point, you can probably define new information for yourself. It is information in a sentence that is not previously known to all, that is not obvious from the rhetorical situation, that is not mentioned prior to that sentence, or that is not recoverable through inferences from earlier material.

Consider again two sentences that I used earlier:

> Bob lives in northern Michigan.
> He happens to enjoy cross-country skiing.

We have already noted that in the second sentence *He* conveys given information. Now we can add that *happens to enjoy cross-country skiing* conveys new information. If these words were whited out, we would not be able to predict them or figure them out on the basis of earlier words. Therefore, in the second sentence of this pair, *He* forms the connection to earlier material and *happens to enjoy cross-country skiing* moves the message into new territory.

Consider two other sentences that we looked at before:

> The pencils had all been sharpened recently.
> The paper was arranged in neat stacks.

We have already noted that *The paper* can be treated as given information since readers can infer it as something closely and frequently related to pencils. Now we can add that *was arranged in neat stacks* conveys new information. If these words were whited out, it would be impossible to predict them or figure them out on the basis of earlier material. For all we would know, the second sentence could appear as follows:

The paper was scattered over the floor.

Taking a closer look at the nature of new information, we see that it is not all of the same kind. We can distinguish brand-new information from unused information. Brand-new information is just that: It is that which writers assume readers have no prior knowledge of. Unused information is that which writers have not introduced into essays but which their readers probably already have some knowledge of. In other words, it is new to the essay but probably known to some extent by the readers.

This distinction usually depends not on the information itself but on who one's readers are. In writing to high-school students about the sound system of language, I could probably safely assume that information about phone-types and phonemes would be brand-new. High-school students would probably be reading about these sounds for the first time. On the other hand, if I were writing to linguists, I would assume when I first brought up information about phone-types and phonemes that the information was unused. These terms have not been mentioned in the essay and are thus not given. But the linguists would know about them, making them unused new information.

Thus, although earlier I wrote that most sentences can be divided into two parts, one conveying given information and one conveying new information, we can now see that the situation is not that simple. Most sentences can indeed be divided into two parts. One part probably bears given information. But that information may be known to all people from experience in the world, may be obvious from the rhetorical situation, may be mentioned in earlier sentences, or may be inferable from earlier material. The other part of the sentence probably conveys new information. But that information may actually be either brand-new or unused, depending on the readers it is intended for. Still, for nearly all our purposes in learning about prose and writing, it will do to think of most sentences as being divisible into two parts, one conveying given information and one conveying new information.

Exercise Five

Each of the following pairs of sentences is followed by a parenthetical description of the readers it is intended for. Look closely at the second sentence in each pair and tell whether it carries new information. If it does, consider the nature of the described readers and tell whether the new information is likely to be brand new or unused.

For example, you might see two sentences such as these:

> Researchers at the Thromby Lab discovered a particle they called a quark.
>
> It is one of the smallest elements of matter.
>
> (Advanced college physics students)

In the second sentence, *is one of the smallest elements of matter* is new information. But for advanced college physics students, it is probably unused, not brand-new, information.

1. The ideas about the deep structure of a sentence were some of Chomsky's most striking early hypotheses.
   The deep structure was the form most available to semantic interpretation.
   (Ninth-graders)
2. The publishers of that journal use only the best materials.
   The paper it is printed on is supposed to last for five hundred years.
   (Journal editors and publishers)
3. Most expert rock-climbers prefer nylon rope.
   It lasts a long time and stretches under pressure, thereby softening most falls.
   (Rock-climbers)
4. The Moore sculpture marks the spot where the first controlled atomic reaction took place.
   The reaction was controlled with rods of graphite.
   (High-school students)
5. The area around Sudbury, Ontario, used to look like the surface of the moon.
   In fact, it was used as a training ground for astronauts.
   (Typical readers of an American newspaper)
6. He fails to distinguish revision from a quick tidying-up of an essay.
   Revision should involve some reconceptualization.
   (Composition teachers)
7. Fishermen use many lures to catch salmon on the Great Lakes.
   Silver spoons are the best to use on overcast days.
   (People who have never fished)

8. The golfer to watch in the upcoming tournament is Gary Player.
   He plays best on challenging courses.
   (Golf fans)
9. He has written several papers on the theme of a sentence.
   The theme is the very first constituent.
   (Linguists)
10. She has written several scholarly papers on Tagalog.
    It has several interesting means for marking sentence topics.
    (Prospective elementary-school teachers in an introductory course on language)

THE INTRODUCTORY CLUSTERS RECONSIDERED

In the light of the foregoing discussion, we should take a closer look at the clusters of sentences that I used to introduce this chapter. All of them have specific problems with given or new information. The first cluster appeared as follows:

> Bruce had to start work very early on Tuesday. Samson is the name of a young dog. Last week Judy was on call at the hospital.

You can now probably describe in detail what is odd about this cluster. As we read the first sentence, we find that it contains only information that is new to us. This is not unusual. Unless the rhetorical situation allows writers and readers to take some things as given, the first sentence in an essay will probably contain only new information. What is odd about these sentences is that both the second and the third sentences also convey only new information. There is no given information that we can use to connect these sentences to each other. Usually in essays, sentences after the first will make connections through given information to sentences preceding them. But here we read what seem to be three unrelated sentences.

The second cluster appeared as follows:

> The President hailed the news that all the leading economic indicators in the United States had gone up. Mr. Reagan was most pleased to announce that the American economy was headed in a positive direction. Our country's chief of staff happily reported that the business climate in the United States was improving.

Here the problem is just the opposite of that of the first cluster. Since the first sentence refers to someone most people know about (the President), it contains some given information. It goes on to convey some new information (*hailed the news that all the leading economic indicators in the United States had gone up*). So far everything is fine. But then the second and third sentences simply repeat what is virtually the same information as conveyed by the first sentence. In other words, they convey only given information. And that usually subverts the purposes of communication and bores readers.

The third cluster appeared as follows:

> Tom is an avid fisherman. Bob also is an avid golfer.

The oddity here is a little more difficult to describe. The key to the trouble is the word *also*. In the second sentence, this word leads us to believe that everything that appears before it (*Bob*) should be new information. And it is. But, in addition, *also* signals that all that appears after it should be given information. We expect to read that *Bob also is an avid fisherman*. Thus we would not be shocked to read just *Bob also* after the first sentence. We would fill in the given information (*is an avid fisherman*) for ourselves. However, what we find (*is an avid golfer*) is mainly new information. And that works against one of the signals sent off by *also*.

The fourth cluster was as follows:

> Barb saw someone. It was Barb who saw James.

Here we find the second kind of *it*-cleft as the second sentence. On the basis of our earlier consideration of the two kinds of *it*-clefts, you probably can describe why this one does not work properly. The keys are the positions of *Barb* and *James*. Since *Barb* appears in the first sentence, it carries given information in the second. But it appears in the position in the *it*-cleft where we expect to find new information. The only new information in the second sentence, obviously, is carried by *James*. The reference to James should trade places with the reference to Barb (*It was James whom Barb saw*). Then these two sentences would work well together.

Finally, we turn to the fifth cluster:

> They are blue. In the closet are my running shoes.

These two sentences violate our expectation of how something normally is introduced into an essay and then is referred to later.

Usually, the first reference will involve a proper name (*Ronald Reagan*) or a full noun phrase (*The President of the United States*). Later references may then take the form of pronouns (*he*). But in the sentences of the fifth cluster, just the opposite happens. First we read a pronoun (*They*), and we have no way of knowing what this refers to. And then we read the full noun phrase (*my running shoes*). The order in which the sentences in this cluster appear can make us wonder whether *They* and *my running shoes* actually refer to the same things. The sentences should appear as follows:

> My running shoes are blue. They are in the closet.

Exercise Six

Something is odd or wrong about each of the following ten clusters of sentences. Using what you know about given and new information, explain the problem in each. Then revise the clusters to correct the problem.

For example, you could see a cluster such as the following:

> Bruce rode his bike a lot last week.
> Bruce traveled by means of his bicycle very extensively last week.

Here the second sentence conveys essentially the same information as the first. It is all given information. To revise it, you would have to add some new information to it: *He saw some interesting tulip farms.*

1. Steve took a trip to Glacier National Park. Martha bought a new car. The electrician installed two new wall sockets.
2. We recently bought a new furnace. Just last week we purchased a new gas home-heating appliance. Not too long ago we invested in a new home-heating unit.
3. They said that they really did not care for the hoagies the deli had on sale. I also jog during the afternoon break.
4. It rained all yesterday afternoon. The sunshine then was brilliant.
5. Without a doubt, that movie is terrifying. Even Big Al was not afraid.
6. Diane loved to take hikes at Starved Rock State Park. Her sons, too, enjoyed racing their dirt bikes.
7. He sprained his knee and had to be taken to the medical center. His wisdom teeth were really bothering him.
8. Unfortunately, they had to have their stomachs pumped. They did not brush after every meal.

9. Did you hear whom Henrietta ran into in Amsterdam? It was Henrietta who ran into Johannes Vander Sma.
10. Erica demanded a new toy. It was Erica who wanted the mechanical barking dog.

TO REVIEW:
GIVEN INFORMATION,
NEW INFORMATION, AND
THEIR ROLE IN COMMUNICATION

Up to this chapter, we have analyzed sentences by dividing them into two parts, the topic and the comment. Now we can add to the analysis, for most sentences contain some given and some new information. Why each of these? The presence of new information is easy to explain, since one of the main functions of language is to convey new information, to increase the knowledge shared by different minds. If sentences convey no new information, we wonder what the point of the communication is. Our first reaction is to say that we do not understand. Our second reaction, probably, is to become bored.

But as we have seen, we also are troubled if we encounter only new information in sentences. Sentences with only new information confuse us. We learn little from them. We might not even be able to understand them.

How do we learn most things? By relating something new to something we already know about. Therefore, most sentences include some given information to link them to earlier sentences or to our memories. You have probably experienced the joy of incorporating bits of new information into mental frameworks that you already possess. In college this happened frequently for me in an art history course that helped me incorporate much new information into what I already knew about cultural movements such as Classicism and Romanticism. As you learn more about expressing given and new information appropriately in your prose, you will be able to participate more skillfully in the processes of communication.

FURTHER READING

Brown, G., and G. Yule (1983), "Information Structure." *Discourse Analysis.* Cambridge: Cambridge University Press.

Chafe, W. L. (1974), "Language and Consciousness." *Language, 50*, 111-133.
Chafe, W. L. (1976), "Givenness, Contrastiveness, Definiteness, Subjects, Topics, and Point of View." In C. N. Li (Ed.), *Subject and Topic* (pp. 25-55). New York: Academic Press.
Dahl, Ö. (1976), "What Is New Information?" In N. E. Enkvist and V. Kohonen (Eds.), *Reports on Text Linguistics: Approaches to Word Order* (pp. 37-49). Turku, Finland: Åbo Akademi.
Prince, E. F. (1981), "Toward a Taxonomy of Given-New Information." In P. Cole (Ed.), *Radical Pragmatics* (pp. 223-255). New York: Academic Press.
Vande Kopple, W. J. (1986), "Given and New Information and Some Aspects of the Structures, Semantics, and Pragmatics of Written Texts." In C. R. Cooper and S. Greenbaum (Eds.), *Studying Writing: Linguistic Approaches* (pp. 72-111). Beverly Hills: Sage Publications.

10

Expressing Given and New Information in Appropriate Places and Forms

---

Again, in any conversation or text, what has gone before constitutes one (constantly growing) context of whatever sentence one is interpreting at the moment. . . .
> —Wendell V. Harris, "Toward an Ecological Criticism: Contextual Versus Unconditioned Literary Theory"

Learning, then, involves a movement from what is already known, or constructed, to what is new and therefore unconstructed.
> —Robert P. Parker, "Writing Courses for Teachers: From Practice to Theory"

The point is that all "new information" is usually integrated into information already known.

> —Teun A. van Dijk, *Text and Context*

Further, the more relevant background knowledge the person has for a given piece of new information, the easier it is to find a representative structural address for it and to retain it.

—Valde Mikkonen, "Cognitive Learning: Research and Practice"

Rather, discourse is an informational hybrid *or an informational* compromise, *whereby each proposition in the chain of discourse adds some information, so that it is not totally tautological and thus informationally redundant, given the pre-existing data base; nor is it totally novel, without any overlap with pre-existing knowledge—and thus unintegrable and the functional equivalent of a contradiction.*

—T. Givón, *Syntax*

Now that we have seen that most sentences contain both some given and some new information, we can move to a guideline about where and in what form the given and new information should usually appear.

THE SEVENTH GUIDELINE

The seventh guideline for clear and coherent prose is as follows: In general, express bits of given and new information in sentences so that it is as easy as possible for readers to use the given-new strategy of comprehension on those sentences. Sentences that facilitate the use of the given-new strategy will strike readers as very readable.

THE GIVEN-NEW STRATEGY OF COMPREHENSION

Researchers have found that when we read a sentence, we usually move through three steps, probably subconsciously. First, we divide the sentence into bits of given and new information. Then we use the given information as an indicator of the point in our memories that we should be attending to. In the sample sentence that we used earlier (*He happens to enjoy cross-country skiing*), *He* connects to the place in our memories where we have stored all that we know about the person to whom *He* refers (Bob). Finally, once we find the appropriate point in memory, we add the new information to it.

But sometimes sentences do not indicate clearly to what point in memory we are to add new information. Sometimes they contain no given information at all. And sometimes they force us to check if there are possible inferences from some of the material in them that we have failed to make. If there is no explicit given information and if it is impossible to infer some given information, then we must add altogether new anchoring points to our memories. Usually, however, sentences will include recognizable bits of given information to show us where in our memories we will be adding new information.

With this discussion as background, we can clearly see some of the main characteristics of sentences that help readers use the given-new strategy of comprehension on them. Some of these we touched on in the discussion of the clusters that introduced Chapter Nine.

In the first place, these sentences should contain some given information. That will enable readers to locate the spot in their memories where they will be adding new information. Second, the given information should be easy to recognize. If it is not, readers will have to spend valuable time trying to figure out what point in their memories to attend to. Third, although not obvious from the description of the given-new strategy, the given information should be expressed in the appropriate form, one that calls the appropriate amount of attention to it. Finally, the given information should usually precede the new information in sentences. Readers proceed best when they first know where they will be adding some new information and then learn the new information itself. I will take up each of these characteristics in turn.

INCLUDING SOME
GIVEN INFORMATION

Occasionally I find students writing sentences that contain no given information. Doing this, of course, keeps readers from connecting the new information to anything. It does not draw readers' attention to a point in their memories that they will modify by adding new information.

The following cluster contains a sentence without given information:

> Preparing for a marathon demands months of sometimes painful efforts and sacrifices. I played baseball for hours on end. Of course, the preparation includes the long training runs marathoners must go through each day. But it also extends to what the runners eat and to how much they sleep.

The sentence without given information should be easy to spot. It is the second one. The only element in the second sentence that could possibly be taken as given is the *I*, since we can infer that the cluster has an author. But since *I* or the author's name does not appear before the second sentence, and since we usually do not take essays as conveying information primarily about the author unless the author alerts us that we should, we do not find it necessary to add a point to our memories for the person that *I* refers to. Thus the second sentence strikes us as being out of place; it seems like an unannounced aside. We wonder what motivated the author to include it (perhaps some connection between the time involved in training for a marathon and the hours spent playing baseball). And the second sentence may even annoy us as we try to figure out how it fits into this cluster. It is worth noting here that if a writer has included a sentence without given information in a piece, that sentence will often be the second one.

If we look at a good deal of clear and effective prose, we will find that in many sentences the given information corresponds to the topic. This is true of *He happens to enjoy cross-country skiing*. In it, *He* (the bearer of given information) is also the topic. Therefore, in this sentence, as in many others, what a sentence is about is actually material that has already been introduced into the essay.

But even when the topics of their sentences convey given information, many writers choose to convey additional given information in those sentences. They think it important to show readers how to connect one sentence to earlier ones. This is particularly important for you to keep in mind when you begin new paragraphs or sections of essays. Some of my students tend to use no given information or too little given information at important junctures in essays rather than too much.

We can use many syntactic structures to convey more given information than we can express in the topic of an independent clause. For example, we can use a prepositional phrase:

> The skier caught an edge of his ski in the snow and fell over three big bumps. *After the fall*, he calmly got up, brushed himself off, and proceeded down the mountain.

We can use a participial phrase:

> John later discovered a principle of humor. *Having discovered it*, he tried telling some jokes.

We can use an infinitive phrase:

> The new word-processing program is easy to use. *To use it*, you need only know how to type.

Or we can use an absolute phrase:

> The two honors students passed that comprehensive test. *The test out of the way*, they began writing their papers.

If you want to express even more given information, either in the topic or outside of it, you can use introductory subordinate clauses. As we saw earlier, many of these (many adverbial clauses, for example) often provide given or background information. Such is true of the adverbial in the second sentence of this pair:

> Early in the afternoon Ruth came up with three excellent ideas for the new advertising campaign. *After she came up with the ideas*, she started to sketch them out for a presentation to her boss.

We can also use adjective clauses to express given information. Often, the adjective clause and the noun that it modifies will serve as the topic of the sentence:

> We have just finished a set of computer programs. *The programs that are now finished* will be easy to install and use.

Finally, we can use noun clauses to express given information. The whole noun clause will usually also function as the topic of the sentence:

Andy apologized to Daniel. *That he did so* really amazed Daniel's parents.

Again, I cannot tell you precisely how much given information to use in sentences. It depends. For readers unfamiliar with your subject matter, you will probably want to use more; with readers who are experts in your subject matter, you will probably be able to use less. In a very formal situation, you will probably choose to use more; in a very informal situation, you will probably want less. So examine carefully the rhetorical situation you are in, and read the works of other writers to see how they responded to their rhetorical situations.

You should remember, however, that you should express some given information in your sentences, most likely in all of your sentences, most likely as the topics of these sentences. That will keep your readers from wondering what one of your sentences is doing in an essay. And it will help them clearly know to which bit of information in their memories they will be adding new information.

Exercise One

For each of the following ten sentences, you should write another sentence that follows it and that is connected to it through given information. Practice including given information in more than just the topics of the sentences that you write. And to do so, practice using all of the syntactic structures we examined earlier.

For example, if you were presented with the sentence *The Harpers toured the steamer that was stationed in Cheboygan*, you could follow it with *After they did so, they decided to drive on to Petoskey.*

1. In one day Steve and Gayle hiked all the way to Grinnel Glacier and back.
2. Diane was appointed to be the new softball coach.
3. With his teaching and coaching responsibilities in the fall, Jack is hardly ever home.
4. Vern and James accepted the contract to paint the entire retirement home.
5. Jon's garden now covers nearly ten acres of land near his home.
6. Within a week Liz was appointed concertmistress of the community orchestra.
7. In the winter Bay View is a deserted village.
8. Police in Harbor Springs had no clues in that notorious murder case.

9. Alan stayed in Rhinelander for only one week.
10. A new nature trail has been laid out in Caldecott Park.

ENSURING THAT YOUR
GIVEN INFORMATION IS IDENTIFIABLE

Occasionally writers include in their sentences information that they think is given but that their readers have difficulty identifying as given. And trying to identify the given can be frustrating. You have all probably experienced such frustration in conversations. In them, people often use pronouns without antecedents and leave their hearers wondering to whom the pronouns refer. Not too long ago I met a friend who said, "She is selling strawberries at fifty cents a quart." My friend assumed that I could treat the *She* as given information, but I had no idea to whom it referred and had to ask, "Who is?" Such use of pronouns also is found occasionally in writing, where it is probably a greater flaw since usually the reader cannot ask the writer about antecedents.

A related problem in writing is usually referred to as vague or unclear pronoun reference. This problem occurs when a writer does not make it clear which one of several possible referents serves as the antecedent for a pronoun. For example, you might encounter a pair of sentences such as these:

Mary Ann hiked the nature trail with Jo.
She suffered at least a dozen mosquito bites.

Although you might suspect that both of these sentences focus on Mary Ann, you could not be absolutely certain that the *She* refers to her, since there are two possible referents for it (Mary Ann and Jo, with Jo mentioned closer to the *She*). When this happens, the given–new strategy is blocked since readers cannot tell to what point in their memories they should add the new information.

But problems with identifying given information are probably most frequent with information that writers expect readers to treat as given on the basis of inferences. Often, depending on the subject matter and the extent of your readers' knowledge of it, readers will not be able to make the inferences that you assume they can.

For instance, on our campus we have a swimming pool in the building that we all call the gymnasium. To those who know our campus and the way we talk about it, the following two sentences make perfect sense together:

I think that they should open the gym in the evenings.

The pool would be very popular.

These sentences make sense together since those who know about the buildings on our campus can infer that the pool mentioned in the second sentence is the one we have as part of our gymnasium building. Those with the knowledge to make the inference can treat *The pool* as conveying given information; therefore, they read these two sentences as a coherent short text. Those without this knowledge, however, might not be able to treat *The pool* as given information and might see these two sentences as unrelated to each other. We can assume, though, that they would work hard to find a connection between these sentences and perhaps would conclude that our gymnasium includes a pool.

One of my assumptions in this book, however, is that we should try to minimize the work that readers have to do on our sentences unless there is good reason for them to do it. And we take large strides toward this goal if we ensure that our readers can make the inferences we expect them to. We have to take special care as we write to those who do not belong to the same cultural subgroup we belong to. Even more, we have to take special care when we write to readers who grew up in entirely different cultures from ours.

Recently I taught a composition class in which I had several students who had only recently moved to the United States from Korea. Several times I lost them as I made a general point in one sentence and then gave a specific example from the culture I know well in a second sentence. I was expecting them to infer the connection between bits of information in these two sentences, but the Koreans had never heard of my specific example and therefore could not use it as given information to connect the two sentences. You should let my errors stand as a warning to you about expecting hearers or readers to identify given information through inferences that are difficult or impossible for them to make. This is yet another area in which analyzing what you can expect your readers to know is essential.

Exercise Two

Read each of the following pairs of sentences and then examine the second sentence in each pair carefully, trying to decide whether what is apparently given information in it might be difficult for readers to identify. Also, if the given information appears to be difficult to identify, explain why.

For example, consider the following sentences:

> Put the knife and the saw away.
>
> It is far too dangerous.

In the second sentence, the writer is treating the *It* as given information. However, readers would not be able to treat it as such since it could point to either the knife or the saw.

1. Joel loves to discover abandoned logging camps.
   He uses only the best aerial photographs.
2. Jason went to the hardware store.
   She walked to the park.
3. Becky and Cindy are going to chaperone students on the trip to Glacier.
   They are eager to leave.
4. Julie and Erica spent the afternoon at Holland State Park.
   She got an excellent tan.
5. The Yankee-Dutch dialect has many colorful words for describing everyday things.
   Vies means something close to odious.
6. The Rapid Rig is a difficult lure to fish with.
   The swivel often causes problems.
7. The Marathon is a very fast cross-country ski.
   The fishscales cause very little friction.
8. Roger needed to buy some new equipment.
   His backsaw and mitre box were broken.
9. They had an excellent day sailing.
   The ropes on the jib never got tangled.
10. The fans roared their disapproval.
    The squeeze bunt had failed.

MARKING GIVEN INFORMATION APPROPRIATELY

Next we move to an area in which errors will not keep readers from using the given-new strategy, but they will cause readers to think that the prose is odd. I indicated in Chapter Nine that once a bit of information appears a second and subsequent times in an essay, it will usually take forms different from what it had on its first appearance. Some of these forms call more attention to the bit of information, or mark it with more force, than do others.

For instance, *The old car with the dented fender* calls more attention to the car than *The old car* does. And that calls more attention to the car than *The car* does. Further, *The car* calls more attention to the car than *It* does. It is difficult to know exactly where on this scale another name for the car (such as *The contraption*) fits, but it probably fits toward the top end. Phrases such as *This car* probably fit in near the middle.

It is not critically important to determine where each word or phrase referring to the car fits on such a scale. It is important, though, to realize that such ranges of referring expressions force us to make a choice each time that we refer to something. And not everyone makes wise choices.

For example, if we were to encounter the following two sentences next to each other in an essay, we would object:

> The older man who visited our class raised several questions.
>
> But the older man who visited our class never took the tests.

We would object that the second sentence refers to the old man with too much force. We expect to read *the man* or *he*.

This same flaw turns up in my students' writing occasionally. Here are two sentences from a student's paper on the language of twins:

> Savic also found some interesting features of twins' language in her study of adult-twin interaction. Savic found that twins tend to direct their utterances toward another person more than non-twins usually do. . . .

To my eye and ear, the second appearance of *Savic* was a heavier reference than my student needed. I was expecting to find *She* there.

Similarly, what follows is a sentence from a student's essay about working as a fisherman in Alaska one summer:

> Once the metal starts to corrode, the metal becomes very weak.

Again, I found the second reference to the metal excessively strong. I would have preferred to find an *it* after the comma.

Sometimes writers make the opposite kind of mistake. That is, they do not mark bits of given information with enough force. This is why some given information is difficult to identify. In the following sentence by one of my students, there is a problem with insufficient marking of given information:

> Finally, when Genie was 13½ years old, Genie's mother sought help for her increasing blindness.

The *her* in this sentence does not mark the appropriate bit of given information (be it Genie or her mother) with enough force. Either Genie's first name or words such as *her own* must appear.

Similarly, in an essay in which the Queen of England is referred to first with *Queen Elizabeth* and then with several *she*'s in a row, after a while—probably after four or five *she*'s—you would intuitively want a reference carrying more force. At that time, you would want the writer to substitute *the Queen* for *she*.

As we approach these kinds of decisions, two general considerations should guide us. First, we must consider how long it has been since a bit of given information has been referred to. If it has just been referred to (in the previous sentence, say) it needs less marking. The slight qualification necessary here is that if a bit of given information has been referred to in several successive sentences with markers that call little attention to the given information, it will require a reference that calls more attention to it. The reason for this is that readers' memories for given information fade slightly with each reference that calls little attention to it, and after a while their memories will have to be renewed. On the other hand, if a bit of given information has not been referred to at all in the last page or two, it will require strong marking when it reappears.

Second, we have to consider potential ambiguities. If a bit of given information could be confused with another bit that is expressed near it, we will have to mark the first when it reappears with more punch than we would otherwise have to. This is the reason that I cannot use *she* after I have written the sentence *Mary Ann hiked the nature trail with Jo*. The *she* could refer to at least two women.

This area of marking given information is another in which we cannot formulate precise rules. We cannot say that after 273 words have come between one reference to something and another reference to it, the second reference has to be three steps up the scale of marking force. However, we can describe some general tendencies in English. Furthermore, I hope that once you know about degrees of force in marking given information, you will read others' and your own writing with new eyes and ears. If you do, you should develop greater skill in marking given information in your own writing.

Exercise Three

Each of the following ten sentences is followed by a pair of sentences, one of which is better than the other as a candidate to follow the original sentence. It is better because it marks given information more skillfully than the other. Select which of the pair of sentences is the preferable one, and tell why.

For example, you might see sentences such as these:

Ex. 1:   The librarian with glasses on a chain around her neck scolded the boys for talking.

Ex. 1a: The librarian with glasses on a chain around her neck seemed really upset.

Ex. 1b: She seemed really upset.

Here Ex. 1b is the preferable candidate to follow sentence Ex. 1. Ex. 1a marks given information (*The librarian with glasses on a chain around her neck*) with too much force.

1. He tried to turn the electric typewriter on.
   1a. But it was broken.
   1b. But the electric typewriter was broken.
2. The President of the United States spent the weekend at Camp David.
   2a. He relaxed after an unusually busy week.
   2b. The President of the United States relaxed after an unusually busy week.
3. Ed and Ken recruited players for a new volleyball league.
   3a. Ed was especially effective.
   3b. He was especially effective.
4. Bob hooked two bass while fishing on Duck Lake.
   4a. After intense battles, the two bass both got away.
   4b. After intense battles, they both got away.
5. Ken and Kathy spent a week in the Ozarks.
   5a. He liked the hiking, while Kathy enjoyed the swimming.
   5b. He liked the hiking, while she enjoyed the swimming.
6. Henie and her sister Jo visited Natchez during spring vacation.
   6a. They had originally planned to go to Charleston.
   6b. Henie and Jo had originally planned to go to Charleston.

7. Jan is the team's fastest miler.
   7a. When she learns to pace herself better, she will be unbeatable.
   7b. When Jan learns to pace herself better, Jan will be unbeatable.
8. Sam let down the anchor.
   8a. But the anchor apparently came off the rope.
   8b. But it apparently came off the rope.
9. Jonathan and Joel helped set up the tent.
   9a. He pounded in the stakes, and Joel sorted out the poles.
   9b. Jonathan pounded in the stakes, and Joel sorted out the poles.
10. The gulls were bobbing on the light swells near the anchored sailboat.
   10a. They were looking for minnows hiding under it.
   10b. The gulls were looking for minnows hiding under the sailboat.

EXPRESSING GIVEN INFORMATION BEFORE NEW INFORMATION

Finally, another characteristic of sentences that helps readers use the given–new strategy on them is that they express given information before new information.

Many of the sample sentences that I have already used express given information before new information. For instance, consider again the second sentence in this pair:

Bob lives in northern Michigan.

He happens to enjoy cross-country skiing.

In the second sentence, *He* carries given information. It connects back to the *Bob* of the first sentence. On the other hand, *happens to enjoy cross-country skiing* is new information. It has not been mentioned earlier, and it is not recoverable from material in the first sentence. In the second sentence, therefore, the given information precedes the new information.

When that happens, you will often find a correspondence between the given information and the topic. This is true of *He happens to enjoy cross-country skiing. He* carries given information, and it is also the sentence topic. Moreover, since we have already learned that the topic usually corresponds to the grammatical subject, we see that in many sentences there is a correspondence among subject, topic, and given information.

In addition, in most sentences the new information and the comment will correspond. In *He happens to enjoy cross-country skiing, happens to enjoy cross-country skiing* is both new information and comment. And since we have already learned that the comment and the grammatical predicate often correspond, we see that in many sentences there is a correspondence among predicate, comment, and new information.

Therefore, a formula equating the subject and topic with the given information, as well as the predicate and comment with the new information, is a good one to use as a touchstone for sentence readability. And even if these correspondences do not hold for a sentence, the sentence should at least keep the given information before the new information.

If new information comes before given information, readers must try to retain the new at the same time that they continue into the sentence in search of the given. When they find the given information, they might have to review the new information to remind themselves of all its details. Such processes take time and drain the energy available for reading.

Trying to adhere to this formula as you think of material to write and as you compose sentences may get in the way of your flow of thought. So I suggest that you do not give most of your attention to the formula in the early stages of your work. But you should increase your attention to it as you revise and polish your sentences.

Many of my students seem to be in a hurry to express their new information in sentences. They express it early and then conclude their sentences with references to given information. The given information probably appears last since, as most people compose, given information is not their main concern. Their main concern is to come up with new information. Thus when they do come up with it, they tend to express it first in their sentences. Perhaps this is inevitable. My students often write sentences such as the following:

> Professing to believe in speaking in tongues but casting doubts on accompanying manifestations is yet another view.
>
> Ability for children to work and develop at their own pace is a fourth advantage for home-schoolers.

In the first of these sentences, *yet another view* carries given information; the sentence should therefore be recast so that it reads, *Yet another view is professing to believe in tongues but casting doubts on accompanying manifestations.* In the second sentence, *a fourth advantage for home-schoolers* carries given information; it should introduce the sentence: *A fourth advantage for home-schoolers is that children can work and develop at their own pace.*

Similarly, many students write independent clauses that move from given to new information, but then they apparently decide that they ought to connect those clauses to earlier material explicitly. So they add on to them a phrase or clause carrying only given information. They begin essays about adjusting to college by describing leaving home and meeting a roommate, and then they include a sentence like this:

> I also had to learn to budget my time, in addition to leaving home and meeting a roommate.

The phrase that concludes this sentence is all given information and should probably introduce the sentence or be dropped. If you do not make changes such as those described in this and the preceding paragraph as you revise, you will leave your readers with sentences that will frustrate them as they use the given–new strategy.

You will also leave them with paragraphs and longer stretches of discourse that are not as coherent as they could be. Here is a short paragraph from one of my students on the subject of light rock and roll:

> Light rock and roll can be as comforting to a college student as classical music can be to a professor. The music played on most rock and roll stations is light rock and roll. Yes, the ideas of sex, alcohol, and violence are brought up in the lyrics of light rock and roll, but country music talks of divorce, booze, and violence too.

This student obviously has more than progressions of given and new information to work on. But both the second and the third sentences have given information about light rock and roll expressed later in them than what is ideal. Notice how much more topically coherent this paragraph becomes if we move those expressions of given information earlier in sentences:

> Light rock and roll can be as comforting to a college student as classical music can be to a professor. Light rock and roll is played on most rock and roll stations. Yes, the lyrics of light rock and roll bring up sex, alcohol, and violence, but country music talks of divorce, booze, and violence too.

As evidence that paragraphs with sentences that move from given to new information are easier to read than those with sentences that move from new to given, consider what happened when I showed many of my students pairs of paragraphs that convey essentially the same information. But all the sentences after the first in one paragraph move from given to new information, while in the second paragraph all those after the first move from new to given information.

For example, one relatively simple paragraph that helps readers use the given–new strategy of comprehension is as follows:

> Currently the Marathon is the best waxless ski for recreational cross-country skiing. Its weight is a mere two pounds. Yet its width allows the skier to break a trail through even the heaviest snow. Its most nearly unique characteristic is the fishscale design for its bottom. The Marathon is almost as effective as most waxable skis. In fact, it is even better than some waxable skis when the snow is very wet. The Marathon can be used with most conventional bindings. However, it works best with the Suomi double-lock. Finally, the Marathon is available in six different colors.

All the information in the first sentence of a passage will often be new to readers. But after the first sentence in this paragraph, each sentence moves from a reference to the ski or one of its characteristics to new information about it or one of its characteristics.

In the variant of this paragraph, the positions of bits of given and new information are reversed:

> Currently the best waxless ski for recreational cross-country skiing is the Marathon. A mere two pounds is its weight. Yet the skier can break a trail through even the heaviest snow with its width. The fishscale design for its bottom is its most nearly unique characteristic. Most waxable skis are only slightly more effective than the Marathon. In fact, some waxable skis are not as good as it when the snow is very wet. Most conventional bindings can be used with the Marathon. However, the Suomi double-lock works best with it. Finally, six different colors are available for the Marathon.

Here again, we would normally have to regard all the information in the first sentence as new. But thereafter each sentence moves from new to given information.

When I asked students to tell me which of these two they found easier to read and follow, they overwhelmingly indicated that they preferred the first, which some had read first and some had read second. They wrote that they favored it since "the main idea comes first, followed by an explanation of the idea," because each of its sentences "lets you know right away what it is about," and because "at the beginning of each sentence there was a general topic." This last reaction is particularly striking since, at the time I asked students to make these judgments, I had not introduced them to the idea of sentence topics.

At the same time, students criticized the second paragraph because it "caused me to look back several times before I could follow it." One said that he "would start to read and then wonder what the sentence is talking about." And another added that he "was held to the end of the sentence to find what the subject is."

Such comments in themselves, I believe, provide good evidence for the advantages of expressing given information before new information in sentences. But there is stronger evidence in what happened when I asked different students to read the second paragraph, remove it from their sight, and then try to write it down in a form as close to the original as possible. When they tried to reproduce the paragraph, many students frequently reversed the order of information in sentences. For example, they read a sentence such as *A mere two pounds is its weight* and wrote *Its weight is a mere two pounds*. They had taken what by then was given information in the paragraph (*Its weight*) and moved it to the beginning of their sentences. They responded precisely as if they were using the given information as a common point of reference as they performed the difficult task of trying to reproduce the second paragraph from memory.

Exercise Four

In each of the following pairs of sentences, examine the second sentence carefully. Tell whether there is both given and new information in it, and, if so, whether the bits of information appear in the order that is easiest to read. If they do not appear in this order, revise the sentence so that the bits appear in the proper order.

For example, consider the following pair of sentences:

The first town on the road leading out of Sault Saint Marie is Brimley. Bay Mills is the second.

In the second sentence, there is both given information (*the second*) and new information (*Bay Mills is*). However, the new information precedes the given. This sentence should ordinarily appear as *The second is Bay Mills.*

1. *The Odyssey* is an excellent example of an epic poem. Epic poems usually are governed by elaborate conventions.
2. That new reader for freshman composition is selling well. Ten dollars and ninety-five cents is its current retail price.
3. Bob and Bruce spent this past summer working on the construction crew in Rocky Mountain National Park. Making trails over divides was their hardest job.
4. She has a marvelous oil painting hanging in her office. It depicts a famous scene in Belgian history.
5. They do not wish to become a chartered student organization. What they want is to remain a group very loosely associated with the university.
6. He cut his hand quite severely with the power saw. The picnic table was covered with blood.
7. The telephone suddenly stopped working. A squirrel had gnawed through the wire.
8. She did not want to sit in the restaurant. To go and hear the group in Preservation Hall was what she wanted to do.
9. Recently several literary critics have been stressing the importance of the context of a work. It is the context that enables readers to make accurate inferences about some of an author's intentions.
10. Who painted the barn? It was the barn that Mickey and Rachel painted.

Exercise Five

In each of the following short paragraphs there are some sentences that do not express given information before new information. Find all such sentences and revise them so that they move from given to new.

For example, if we inserted a sentence such as *Most varieties of ski boots can be used with the Marathon* into the earlier paragraph that has the Marathon ski or a characteristic of it as given information in each sentence after the first, that sentence would express new information before given information. It should be revised to read *The Marathon can be used with most varieties of ski boots.*

1. Research Writing is probably the most valuable course for college students. The assignments for this course are three short expository essays and two long, documented research papers. Thus the course requires a great deal of students' time, often too much, in their opinions. But future success in college is almost synonymous with passing Research Writing. Some of the benefits of the course are gaining a greater familiarity with the library and developing organizational skills, analytic ability, and smooth writing style. Some of its disadvantages are cramped fingers, bloodshot eyes, and irritability before paper deadlines. Only freshmen may take Research Writing.

2. The cello is one of the four main members of the violin family. It is about twice as long as a standard-sized violin. Probably the best cellos ever made were built by Antonio Stradavari, whose name is synonymous with the apex of quality in stringed instruments. The cello was first used as a solo instrument by Gabrielli in the seventeenth century. However, it was not used in a concerto until the eighteenth century. Today, an ever-growing role in the orchestra is played by the cello.

3. One movie that really appealed to teenagers was "Star Wars." It included countless zany and exciting special effects. The light saber was one of the more impressive of these. This versatile weapon once was used by Jedi Knights, who were charged with maintaining order and justice in the galaxies. But order and justice were threatened by vile creatures, most of whom were led by Darth Vader. To destroy all the planets that refused to yield to the emperor was his primary goal.

A CLOSER LOOK AT
SOME SYNTACTIC FORMS

In terms of what we now know about given information, new information, and the given–new strategy of comprehension, it is interesting to look back at the *what*-cleft and the *it*-clefts, for these forms lead us to treat certain bits of information as given.

The *what*-cleft moves from given to new information. When people write a sentence such as, *What I need now is a laser printer*, they are treating the *What I need now* as given information. They act as if their needing something is in the air. And almost always what writers treat as given will be known to readers from the context. At the same time, writers are treating *a laser printer* as new information. They assume that their readers do not know about it. In fact, they are

actually sensing that their readers think they need something else—
say a new pen—when in fact they need a laser printer.

The first kind of *it*-cleft also moves from given to new information.
Often writers produce sentences such as *Our student teachers have
plenty of courage. And it is courage that they will need most in the
approaching semester.* When they produce *it*-clefts such as these, they
are repeating a word (*courage*), thereby making it given, and then
they are moving on into significant new information (*that they will
need most in the approaching semester*).

The second kind of *it*-cleft, however, does not move from given to
new information. When writers produce sentences such as *It was
Timmy who ate the kiwi fruit*, they are presupposing that someone ate
the kiwi fruit. The *it*-cleft functions to pick out the person who did it,
and that identity (*Timmy*) is new information.

Since this order of information is the reverse of the order that I
earlier said helped readers use the given-new strategy of comprehension, is it wrong? No. As we have seen, this kind of *it*-cleft is
produced only when speakers or writers feel some pressure. They
feel that they have to select the correct entity or thing from several
candidates, or they feel that they have to correct a mistaken view by
providing some new information. In all cases, though, they feel that
they have to convey the new information quickly. And that urgency
justifies expressing the new information before the given, especially
since the given is usually so apparent that it could be omitted.

This kind of *it*-cleft is sometimes used by writers of fiction for
special purposes. For example, John le Carré begins *The Little
Drummer Girl* with this *it*-cleft:

> It was the Bad Godesberg incident that gave the proof, though the
> German authorities had no earthly means of knowing this (p. 3).

In the novel's first sentence, we are catapulted into the fictional
world. The Bad Godesberg incident gave the proof of something,
which the sentence treats as being given information to us. However,
we have no idea what the Bad Godesberg incident even was, and the
only way we can get an idea is to read on. Thus le Carré draws us
into his fictional world and gives us reason to explore it.

Seeing how le Carré does this helps us see more clearly how
writers can use *what*-clefts and the second kind of *it*-cleft unethically,
for whenever these forms appear in a passage, they lead us to think
that some information is given.

For instance, if we read *What they want is a new diet soft drink*, we take it as given that they do indeed want something. We take *What they want* as given information.

Similarly, if we read *It is his forgetfulness that makes him a poor teacher*, we take it as given that he is a poor teacher. We take *that makes him a poor teacher* as given information.

As we saw in Chapter Five, nothing is inherently wrong in using forms that lead readers to take some information as given. Something is wrong, however, when that information is not true and when it might lead readers to distorted views of things or to harmful actions. We must be careful, therefore, that the information we treat as given in various cleft forms deserves to be viewed as given by readers.

Exercise Six

Although each of the following sentences appears here out of context, each leads readers to take some information as given. Tell what is treated as given in each sentence, and be prepared to discuss whether the writer who decides to use any one of these might be close to an unethical action.

For example, consider the following sentence:

What makes high-school seniors insufferable is their immaturity.

In this sentence, *What makes high-school seniors insufferable* is treated as given information. This sentence is based upon a lie, since it takes as given the gross generalization that all high-school seniors are insufferable.

1. What the college needs is a vision for its future.
2. What makes Mac Flecknoe's poetry great is its satiric edge.
3. What justifies kicking them out of class is their bad attitude toward their peers.
4. What made the bombings necessary was the terrorism around the world.
5. What he lacks is a sense of humor.
6. It is her conceit that makes everyone dislike her.
7. It is the welfare of the country that justifies apartheid.
8. It is sheer laziness that keeps people on welfare.
9. It is unadulterated pragmatism that makes today's college students such shallow human beings.
10. It is egocentrism that makes Americans disagreeable to others.

TO REVIEW:
HELPING READERS USE THE
GIVEN-NEW STRATEGY OF
COMPREHENSION

Chapters Nine and Ten show that sentences express both some given and some new information. The given information appears early to allow readers to connect sentences with material they already know. The new information appears in order to fulfill an important function of language: conveying information that was previously unknown to people and thereby expanding their knowledge of the world.

This chapter also shows how much care writers need to take with the given and new information in their sentences. They must ensure that readers can recognize the information that they treat as given. They must mark bits of given information with the appropriate degree of force. And almost always they should express the given information before the new information. If they do these things, their readers will be able to use the given-new strategy of comprehension well.

This chapter also connects to Chapters Two and Three, since it shows that the given information and the topic often correspond, as do the new information and the comment. Thus now I can add that as you consider what to topicalize in a sentence, in most cases you make the best choice when you topicalize what is given information.

FURTHER READING

Carpenter, P. A. and M. A. Just (1977), "Integrative Processes in Comprehension." In D. Laberge and S. J. Samuels (Eds.), *Basic Processes in Reading: Perception and Comprehension* (pp. 217–241). Hillsdale, N. J.: Lawrence Erlbaum.

Givón, T. (1983), "Topic Continuity in Discourse: An Introduction." In T. Givón (Ed.), *Topic Continuity in Discourse: A Quantitative Cross-Language Study* (pp. 1–41). Amsterdam: John Benjamins.

Goodin, G. and K. Perkins (1982), "Discourse Analysis and the Art of Coherence." *College English, 44*, 57–63.

Haviland, S. E. and H. H. Clark (1974), "What's New? Acquiring New Information as a Process in Comprehension." *Journal of Verbal Learning and Verbal Behavior, 13*, 512–521.

Prince, E. F. (1978), "A Comparison of Wh-Clefts and *It*-Clefts in Discourse." *Language, 54*, 883–906.

Scinto, L. F. M. (1978), "Relation of Eye Fixations to Old–New Information of Texts." In J. W. Senders, D. F. Fisher, and R. A. Monty (Eds.), *Eye Movements and the Higher Psychological Functions* (pp. 175–194). Hillsdale, N. J.: Lawrence Erlbaum.

Vande Kopple, W. J. (1982), "Functional Sentence Perspective, Composition, and Reading." *College Composition and Communication, 33*, 50–63.

11

Avoiding Unnecessary Given Information and Words That Carry No Information (Avoiding Wordiness)

Heat is in proportion to the want of true knowledge.
—Laurence Sterne, *Tristram Shandy*

Modern English, it seems to me, is slack instead of taut, verbose and not concise. . . .
—Kenneth Grayston, "Confessions of a Biblical Translator"

The clearest or most obvious sort or kind of way to multiply words is never to say anything just once.

—Laurence Perrine, "Fifteen Ways to Write Five Hundred Words"

> *A sentence should contain no unnecessary words, a paragraph no unnecessary sentences, for the same reason that a drawing should have no unnecessary lines and a machine no unnecessary parts.*
>
> —William Strunk, Jr., and E. B. White,
> *The Elements of Style*

> *Writing improves in direct ratio to the number of things we can keep out of it that shouldn't be there.*
>
> —William Zinsser, *On Writing Well*, Third Edition

We should consider one additional guideline, another one that relates to the proper functioning of the given-new strategy of comprehension and that I could have included among the subpoints of Chapter Ten. But since most writers fail to follow this guideline at one time or another, and since such failures frustrate and irritate readers, I will allot to this guideline an entire chapter.

THE EIGHTH GUIDELINE

One good way to understand this guideline is to examine prose that does not follow it. When writers fail to follow the eighth guideline, they produce prose such as this:

The current interest rate as of today for home mortgages is basically nine percent. That is, each and every person who has hopes and desires of owning a home should be able to find and secure a loan at a rate of something like nine percent. In the light of the undeniable fact that the prime rate, that which banks charge their best loan customers, has recently shown an obvious and noticeable tendency to rise, however, one should be able to anticipate in advance that a rise in the mortgage rate will soon be assured beyond a shadow of a doubt. In a very real sense, then, all those who have thought about and considered buying a house probably should immediately apply for a loan at this precise point in time. For it is a certainty that as the mortgage rate rises, those who fundamentally qualify for loans become fewer and fewer in number.

I hope that after you have read this paragraph only once, you can see how inflated it is. I also hope that you can anticipate the content of the eighth guideline: In general, avoid using words that unnecessarily repeat given information or that carry no real information at all.

Following this guideline should help you avoid most sources of wordiness in your prose, for as we will see, most cases of wordiness occur when a writer repeats given information without a good reason or uses words that carry no information at all. In so doing, the writer adds words but no new meaning to an essay.

AVOIDING UNNECESSARY REPETITION OF GIVEN INFORMATION

We must remember that repeating some given information in sentences is usually necessary to connect them to earlier ones and to make the set of sentences coherent. What we are concerned with here, however, is repeated given information that is not needed for the coherence of passages. It is repeated for no good reason.

Writers break this guideline most noticeably when they produce independent sentences that convey only given information. That is, at one point they include a particular sentence, and then later they use the same or virtually the same sentence again.

My students succumb to this temptation quite often. To be fair to them, I should add that I notice sentences that are identical or virtually identical to earlier ones most often in essays written in response to questions on examinations. Students apparently feel great pressure to fill as many pages as possible when they write essay answers, and so they sometimes write the same thing over and over. And to some extent, teachers are responsible for this. Few students that I have met say that they are comfortable making and defending points as concisely as possible. They say that over the years their teachers have usually rewarded them for long answers and not for concise ones.

Quite frequently, though, I also find sentences with only given information in essays that students have had time to think about and revise. For example, in a paper on language development, one of my students sums up the material of two pages by noting that environmental factors influence children as they develop language. Then she asks whether hereditary or genetic factors play a role. One sentence later she repeats all this information: "The influences of environment contribute significantly, but what about the biological conditions?"

Similarly, toward the end of a paper on dialects, another of my students writes that there is still a great deal to be discovered about dialects. About a half-page later she writes, "After studying some of the aspects of dialects, I find that there is still much more to be learned."

Finally, in an essay about how those who survived Nazi concentration camps kept their sanity, another of my students makes the claim that prisoners kept their sanity by going about their business day by day, and by not allowing themselves to think about the horrors around them. The point is interesting and probably true. However, the trouble is that my student makes the point about five times in an essay of approximately three hundred words—near the beginning, between paragraphs in the middle, and at the end.

Often writers will not repeat a sentence word for word. Instead, they reword it so that if readers are not alert, they might not realize that they have seen the information before. At one point in an essay they might read a sentence such as *Those who apply for financial aid from the university must prove that their families are supporting them as fully as possible.* Later in the same essay they might read, *It is imperative that applicants for university-controlled monetary grants and scholarships certify that they can receive no additional financial support from their families.*

Does this gimmick seem familiar? I suppose that at one time or another we have all taken the substance of one sentence in an essay, reworded it without changing it appreciably, and then added it to the same essay, probably as a desperate move to make the essay longer.

Obviously, doing all this frustrates the given–new strategy, for readers are searching in sentences for new information and finding none. When this happens, it does not take them long to get bored with the writing and to put it aside. Sentences with only given information usually work against one of the fundamental aims of discourse, that of communicating new information to readers. Generally we should make each of our sentences work to achieve this aim.

Sometimes, of course, what looks like a mere repetition of the information in a sentence is not quite that. One of my students introduced a paper on theories of Bible translation by writing that "The Bible is the most translated book in the world." She followed this sentence with one whose meaning seems almost identical to it: "No other book has been translated so often and into so many languages." Is this all given information? Not really, for the second sentence adds new information about how we are to interpret the words *most translated book*. Could these two sentences be combined? Yes, but then the writer would lose some of the emphatic and catchy conciseness of the first sentence.

In other situations writers repeat all or nearly all of the information from an earlier sentence and then add just a bit or two of new information to it. They do this particularly when they are trying to explain difficult material to readers. They try to shed a slightly different light on given material in hopes of making it more understandable.

But why would writers merely repeat given information? One perfectly legitimate reason is that they have important points they wish to stress. Another related one is that they have to mark very clearly the way for readers at major junctures or turning points in essays. The justification for sentences used in this way grows stronger as essays grow longer and more complex. And still another possible justification is that a repetition can contribute to a pleasing rhythm or give a firm sense of closure to an essay or one of its main parts.

Too often, though, sentences with only given information cannot be defended. Often they appear when writers feel the need to pad their essays. Sometimes they bespeak insufficient confidence on the part of writers about their readers' powers of understanding. And they can reveal writers who are overstating their case. I will never forget the sting I felt after I got one of my first graduate-school essays back. After some compliments, the professor wrote that he wondered why I felt compelled to make my main point so often. He wrote that he felt as if I did not trust him to follow my prose or as if he were reading someone who kept shouting how important his ideas were.

In sum, then, occasionally you will be able to justify a sentence that conveys only given information. Read accomplished writers to see how often and in what situations they slow things down and include such a sentence. More often than not, however, such sentences should be revised or eliminated.

Similar comments apply to other structures besides independent clauses or sentences. As we have seen, we generally need some given information to bind sentences together. But sometimes writers repeat more given information than they need to. Sometimes in their sentences they include dependent clauses that unnecessarily repeat given information.

As we have seen, many adverbial clauses convey given information. They establish strong and clear connections between sentences. This is evident in the following two sentences from one of my students (with the adverbial italicized): "I stress the important effect that our words have on others. *Because of the effect that our words can have on others*, I emphasize that the language arts should be taken seriously."

Sometimes such connections will strike readers as being stronger and more explicit than the situation warrants. Especially when writers use an adverbial clause carrying only given information in one sentence after the next, they can give readers the impression that they believe readers cannot follow their prose without a great deal of help. How long before prose such as the following (in which the adverbials appear in boldface) becomes wearisome to you?

> Students are responsible for ensuring that they complete all the stages of the registration process. They should begin by making an appointment with their academic advisor. **Once they have made an appointment with their advisor**, they should make sure that they keep that appointment. **When they meet for that appointment**, they should ask all the questions that have arisen during the past semester. **After they ask all their questions**, they should suggest courses that they wish to take. **As soon as they receive permission to register for these courses**, they should proceed to the registrar's office. **Once they get to that office**, they will be expected to ask for class cards and to make a deposit on their tuition charges.

It would be easy to prolong this, but you get the point. The writer of this paragraph seems overly concerned with connecting one directive or bit of advice to the next. Perhaps some students need and welcome so much given information repeated in the adverbial clauses. When I am following directions about how to do something very difficult, I often appreciate adverbial clauses carrying primarily given information. They give me little signs of accomplishment as I move from one step to the next. But in the case of the paragraph used above, most readers would probably feel patronized by it and resent it.

Sometimes writers misuse adjective clauses in a similar way. At one point they make a claim such as *We must preserve our state's wetlands*. Then a few sentences later they repeat that information in an adjective clause. They may write, *Our state's wetlands, which we must preserve, are found primarily in the north-central region.* In such cases the impression they can give is that they are simply reasserting something that they ought to provide evidence for. And that can lead readers to suspect that the writers cannot provide the necessary evidence.

Phrases, too, can unnecessarily repeat given information. For example, I often notice writers using participial and prepositional phrases at the beginnings of their sentences to repeat unnecessary given information. The sample paragraph used above could appear not with adverbial clauses bearing unnecessary given information but with participial and prepositional phrases (in boldface) doing so:

> Students are responsible for ensuring that they complete all the steps of the registration process. They should begin by making an appointment with an academic advisor. **Having made an appointment with an advisor**, they should make sure that they keep that appointment. **Upon meeting for that appointment**, they should ask all the questions that have arisen during the past semester. **After asking all their questions**, they should suggest courses that they wish to take. **Upon receiving permission to register for these courses**, they should proceed to the registrar's office. **At the registrar's office**, they will be expected to ask for class cards and to make a deposit on their tuition charges.

Finally, writers can break the guideline about wordiness by repeating individual words in the same sentence. Occasionally I find a sentence such as this in a student's writing: *Then they had to pack their gear and leave Jackson Glacier then.* Such sentences are probably the results of absentmindedness or haste.

More often, though, I read sentences in which the repetition of a word is not quite so obvious. I am thinking of sentences such as these: *On his birthday he received a bike for which he had been whining for* and *Who is the only other teacher with four classes other than Mr. Sepanic?* In these cases, however, careful editing should catch and delete the repeated words.

More often still I find sentences in which one word is followed by one or more near or exact synonyms. Sometimes near synonyms can add new and interesting slants on things. But often they serve no useful purpose and should be edited out. The following sentence from one of my students should be edited at the end of its comment: "The insignificant impact of theory on the teaching of writing should not be too startling, surprising, or shocking."

As a footnote to this discussion, I must add that when you do include new information in sentences, your readers will almost always expect you to go on to elaborate on it. They will expect you to make it given information and then to include some new information about it. Bringing up new information and then dropping it altogether can frustrate readers as much as writing sentences with no new information at all will.

Some examples should make this clearer. One of my students once wrote an interesting paper on the language of sport. At one point he makes the claim that the language used in the media covering sports is a distinct subvariety of the English language. As I read, I was immediately interested. But the paper includes nothing more on this. It goes on to show how several metaphors originated in the language associated with sports. I felt as if someone had made me a promise and then immediately broken it.

In another instance, a student writing an informal essay about nicknames concluded by noting that her own nickname as a child was "Slim Jen" and that this nickname shows how they can be both fun and hurtful. However, she does not explain precisely how this name was fun and yet hurtful. Readers can guess, but she probably should have expanded on her point and kept them from wondering about it.

Exercise One

In each of the following short paragraphs, there is a sentence with only given information. Find these sentences, and discuss with others whether any of them could be justified.

For example, consider the following short paragraph:

> The hunters and trappers of the Old West had to be tough merely to survive. They had to be tough just to stay alive. But toughness is a concept that they probably would have found alien. Toughness begins

to live as a concept only when there is softness to contrast it to. And these men's lives allowed no softness whatsoever.

Here the offending sentence is the second one. Some of the others contain a good deal of given information, but they also add bits of new information or show new relationships between bits of given information. The second does neither of these things. And it is hard to imagine a compelling argument for so much repetition in such a short paragraph.

1. The trip around Lake Superior is a treasure of things and places to see. The western shore of the lake, especially in Minnesota, is composed of impressive headlands and fine agate beaches. Near Thunder Bay is Kakabeka Falls, one of the more impressive yet lesser known waterfalls in North America. It is as impressive as any waterfall in North America, but not too many people know about it. Wawa is the home of the famous statue of a Canada goose. And not too far south of Wawa is the Agawa river and canyon. The canyon reminds people of terrain in the Rocky Mountains.

2. John's favorite vacation spot is the coast of Maine. Even though it is often wrapped in a layer of fog, it still offers him many things to do. He loves waiting for low tides and then exploring tidal pools. He most enjoys finding sea cucumbers. They are his favorite creatures to find. But he also enjoys exploring the beaches, jumping from boulders to rock shelves, watching for unusual pieces of driftwood. Finally, at times he likes to sit on the beach and gaze out to sea. Before him glide great yachts, sails straining to fly. Before him also clamor old lobster boats, winches whining as they haul pots through sixty feet of water.

3. If you visit Wolverine Basin, you should probably take the trail to Calypso Cascade. The trail is neither long nor steep. There is nothing particularly dangerous about it at all. But from the foot of the cascade you can see a most dangerous spot indeed. At the top of the falls the stream narrows to about sixteen feet. And through the years the granite boulders that hem it in have grown green with algae. Many people with just the right touch of recklessness think that they can jump from one bank to the other at the top of the falls and impress all those watching below. They have tried, and they have failed. They either slip as they leap, do not jump far enough, or slip as they land. In any case, they become part of the cascade, being bounced from one level to the next just as pieces of wood and stones are. Therefore, be warned. No one should try to jump across Calypso Cascade. Jumping the cascade is a feat not to be attempted.

_____

Exercise Two

In the following passage many elements—clauses, phrases, and words—convey given information. Some of these are probably unnecessary. Find all these elements and then decide whether they are necessary or whether they should be shortened.

For example, consider the following two sentences:

> You should begin by sorting the clothes by color. After you have sorted the clothes by color, measure out two cups of detergent and then pour the measured detergent into the machine.

In the second sentence, the introductory adverbial clause conveys given information that is probably unnecessary in these directions, which are very easy to follow. This clause could be replaced by a *Then*. The words *measured detergent* also carry given information. This information is necessary, but it probably should be conveyed by the pronoun *it*.

1. Commencement Day is so hectic that the occasion is almost spoiled for many graduates. This very hectic day begins with a graduation breakfast, and at this breakfast the president of the college speaks, the president of the alumni association speaks, and the president of the senior class speaks. After the presidents of the college, the alumni association, and the senior class speak, the graduates get to enjoy some entertainment. Earlier in the year they chose their favorite entertainers from among all those students in their class, and now these selected students sing, these selected students play instruments, and these selected students present humorous skits for entertainment.

   After enjoying the entertainment provided by students in their class, the graduates stream over to the gymnasium for rehearsal for graduation. At this rehearsal for graduation, the registrar and his assistants explain all the details of the upcoming graduation ceremony. The graduates are invited to ask questions, and once they ask their questions, they may leave the gymnasium, where the graduation rehearsal is held, and enjoy lunch with their families and friends.

   After lunch with their families and friends, they must get ready for the commencement ceremony itself, the event for which they have been working for. The processional for the graduation ceremony involves administrators, faculty members, and the graduates all marching in a formal procession. They then all listen to a speaker who has been selected for the commencement ceremony by the president of the college.

Once the graduates have received their degrees in the commencement ceremony, they then proceed to a post-commencement reception for graduates, their families and friends, and faculty members. At this reception the graduates get a chance to introduce their friends and relatives to their teachers, who also attend the reception. After they introduce their friends and relatives to their teachers, the graduates head back to their rooms to finish packing after graduation. Only as they finish packing in their rooms do they have a little time to reflect on what they have accomplished in leading up to their hectic graduation day.

AVOIDING UNNECESSARY REPETITIONS OF IMPLIED INFORMATION

So far we have examined wordiness that results from the unnecessary repetition of given information in independent sentences, dependent clauses, phrases, and words. Now we examine a less noticeable but still troublesome source of wordiness.

To approach this source, consider the following sentences, each of which was written by one of my students:

Personally, I feel that both men and women are equally guilty of gossip.

The child relies quite heavily on the surrounding environment to guide him in his speech development.

What is troublesome about these sentences? It is not that they repeat words. Rather, it is that they include words with meanings that are clearly implied by other words. This is not much different from repeating previously used words, since, as we saw in Chapter Nine, information that is implied functions as given information.

If you wish to write *I feel* (which many teachers warn against because their students often write *I feel* when they mean *I think*), you do not need to include *Personally*. The word *I* already implies that meaning. Similarly, if you use the word *environment*, you need not add *surrounding*. *Environment* implies the meaning of *surrounding*. In other words, both of the sample sentences include words with meanings clearly implied by other words. Such repetitions of implied information are normally called redundancies.

Redundant Pairs of Words

Several kinds of redundancies appear in prose that is not carefully edited. One of these is frequently called the redundant pair of words. Such a pair appears in this sentence from one of my students: "What has been accomplished and learned in experiments with primates in the last few years is indeed impressive."

It is certainly possible that in some situations a writer could use *accomplished* and *learned* to mean different things. In this sentence, however, my student is using these two words in such a way that the meaning of one of them includes or clearly implies the meaning of the other. Here accomplishing something means learning something. Therefore, my student would have been wise to edit out one of these words before submitting her paper.

This latter claim would also be true of most uses of the following pairs of words:

> *aid* and *abet*
>
> *basic* and *fundamental*
>
> *concerned* and *worried*
>
> *esteemed* and *honored*
>
> *first* and *foremost*
>
> *full* and *complete*
>
> *hopes* and *desires*
>
> *hope* and *trust*
>
> *imagine* and *picture*
>
> *kill* and *exterminate*
>
> *knowledge* and *awareness*
>
> *many* and *numerous*
>
> *moan* and *groan*
>
> *old* and *ancient*
>
> *optimize* and *maximize*
>
> *organizations* and *groups*
>
> *personality* and *character*
>
> *primary* and *main*
>
> *significant* and *important*
>
> *thankful* and *grateful*
>
> *troublesome* and *bothersome*

various and *sundry*

vexing and *irritating*

These pairs occur to us too easily. Very recently I caught myself writing this examination question: "What impediments and hindrances to effective teaching of English do you see in the system of secondary education in the United States?" Fortunately, I was working on a word processor and could erase *and hindrances.*

Redundant Modifiers

Another kind of redundancy occurs in this sentence: *What positive benefits did you experience in the semester of student teaching?* In this kind of redundancy, an unnecessary modifier (usually an adjective, adverb, or prepositional phrase) is associated with another word (usually a noun or a verb). The modifier is unnecessary since its meaning is clearly implied by the noun or verb. In the sample sentence, the meaning of *benefit* clearly implies the meaning of *positive*. The word *positive*, therefore, should be edited out.

Some examples of groups of words in which a redundant modifier is associated with a noun are as follows:

advance planning

architecture of the building

authentic truths

autobiography of her life

basic essentials

basic fundamentals

complete overview

consensus of opinion

final completion

final conclusion

final outcome

landscape of the grounds

memories of the past

monetary fine

new innovation

predictions for the future

recurrent motifs

self-confidence in himself

tall skyscraper

terrible tragedy

troublesome problem.

Some examples of groups of words in which a redundant modifier is associated with a verb are as follows:

anticipate in advance

bisect into two parts

circle around

connect together

continue further

convince totally

finish completely

fuse together

imagine in your mind

install in

kill completely

raise up

recoil back

repeat again

say in this statement

scrutinize carefully

sever off

share in common

shuttle back and forth

start in the first place.

Redundant Classifications

The final kind of redundancy that we will examine appears in this sentence: *Anglers out at daybreak for the opening of trout season were many in number.* Here the trouble comes from *many in number.* The writer uses a specific word (*many*) and then adds to it words that supply the more general classification into which it fits (*in number*). But the meaning of *many* clearly implies the meaning of *in number*. Hence *in number* should be dropped.

Some other common phrases that contain redundancies of this sort appear below. You should be able to add to this list quite extensively by changing the more specific item in each phrase:

attractive in appearance
audible to the ear
calm in temperament
coarse to the touch
light in weight
light in complexion
long in distance
long in length
moral in character
putrid in odor
rolling in terrain
round in shape
stubborn in nature
tall in height
visible to the eyes.

Exercise Three

Each of the following sentences contains one or more kinds of redundancy. Find each redundancy and identify it by kind.

For example, in *My final and concluding point is that professors ought to be concerned about the political implications of what they teach* contains the redundant pair of words *final and concluding.*

1. At approximately 7:00 a.m. in the morning, they spotted a bird that was scarlet in color.
2. Each and every graduate will soon be called by the alumni office for donations.
3. Mix the two liquids together in a room that is well ventilated.
4. The speaker reiterated again that the students had been asking the wrong questions all along.
5. That movie struck them as endless in length and poorly directed.
6. Once you have completed the necessary prerequisites, you may register for the seminar in methods.

7. Those student teachers were patient in nature.
8. The campus police ordered the protestors to cease and desist assembling together on campus.
9. Their maple sugar was sweeter to the taste than that of any other manufacturer in the state.
10. They first sought the true facts, and then they wrote a major and noteworthy news story.

AVOIDING PRESENTING INFORMATION IN MORE WORDS THAN NECESSARY

Another way in which writers break the guideline about wordiness is by using more words than they need to convey a certain bit of information. The information is necessary; it may even be a part of the new information in a sentence. But the point is that it could be conveyed in fewer words than the writers actually use.

For instance, one of my students recently turned in a term paper that includes this sentence: "People believe that women talk more than men due to the fact that women are expected to be quiet." Here the information carried by "due to the fact that" is necessary; it makes an important logical connection.

However, essentially that same information could be conveyed in only one word, a *because* or a *since*. And unless you are trying to imitate the style of a bureaucrat, you should try to write as economically as possible. As you edit, therefore, change clusters of words such as *due to the fact that* to shorter equivalents such as *because*.

Exercise Four

Below are several groups of words similar to *due to the fact that*. That is, they convey information that could be expressed in fewer words, often in only one word. Try to think of a one- or two-word equivalent for each of these groups.

For example, the information conveyed by *for all time and eternity* could also be conveyed by *forever*, and that conveyed by *at the same time* could also be conveyed by *simultaneously*.

1. at the conclusion of
2. along the lines of
3. at this juncture of maturization

4. at this point in time
5. at this point in space
6. by means of
7. designed so that
8. despite the fact that
9. during the time that
10. for the purpose of
11. in a careful manner
12. in a position to
13. in many cases
14. in regard to
15. in similar ways
16. in the area of
17. in the event that/of
18. in the final analysis
19. in the light of the fact that
20. in the not too distant future
21. in the present circumstances
22. is able to
23. of importance
24. on the basis of
25. on the grounds that
26. regardless of the fact that
27. render inoperative
28. the reason being
29. the reason that
30. the manner in which
31. the question as to whether
32. the way in which
33. to make a long story short
34. until such time as
35. was of a mind to
36. was of the belief that
37. with respect to
38. with the possible exception of

Exercise Five

Write five sentences, using in each as many as possible of the clusters listed above or discovered by you. Your goal is to produce five sentences that are wordy because they contain more words than necessary to convey a certain body of information.

For example, you might come up with sentences such as *In the light of the fact that we had only two weeks to prepare for this assignment, at this point in time we argue for an extension until such time as we can complete the assignment without inconvenience.*

AVOIDING WORDS THAT
CARRY NO REAL INFORMATION

The last way to break the guideline on wordiness that we will consider involves using words that convey no information at all. This is not a matter of given and new information; it is a matter of using words that contribute no substance to an essay. They are thus often called deadwood and are a kind of insult to readers.

Deadwood appears in this sentence: *The point I wish to make is essentially that people learn best that which they must teach to others.* The word that I am concerned with is *essentially*. *Essentially* has meaning; it can convey information. Writers will use it to contrast the essence of something to the surface or appearance of that same thing. In this sentence, however, it does not mean that. In fact, here it probably conveys no information at all. When writers use words such as *essentially* in this way, they do so probably because they are depending on filler words in writing, just as we all do occasionally in speech, because they are trying to pad an essay, or because they are hoping to sound learned and powerful.

Since words such as *essentially* can carry important meanings in some contexts but little or no meaning in others, we have to take great care to make sure that we use them when they are necessary but delete them when they are not. Other words that often fall into this category appear below:

actually	degree
angle	facet
appearance	factors
aspect	feature
basically	instance
character	level
condition	manner
definitely	nature

quite	state
rather	type
really	various
situation	very
somewhat	virtually

In addition, some clusters of words often function as deadwood. Some of the more common of these follow:

all things considered
as a matter of fact
in a manner of speaking
in great measure
in the final analysis
in the long run
more or less
needless to say
to a certain degree

Exercise Six

Each of the following ten sentences contains a word or a group of words that should be suspected of carrying no information. Find these ten words or clusters of words. Then try to write a sentence for each in which it does carry information.

For example, in *Strictly speaking, the meeting is set for noon*, the words *strictly speaking* carry no information. However, they do in a sentence such as *Strictly speaking, "structuralism" can refer to several different theoretical movements*.

1. Fundamentally, all the questions on the examination for the Shakespeare course tested recall, not interpretation.
2. The provisional schedule, as it were, requires all faculty members to be on campus until the last day in May.
3. For all intents and purposes, they were very upset by all the instances of plagiarism that they had discovered.
4. The change in the curriculum, in a very real sense, went into effect in the fall of 1972.

5. Intense stimulation will contribute to the area of growth in creativity.
6. It is rarely the case that students forget about their examinations.
7. The skills of analysis, as with the case of the art of clear communication, are difficult to learn.
8. Virtually, the community voted to allow the radical group to screen its new promotional film in the community center.
9. The Wolverines have won the regional title for ten consecutive years, generally speaking.
10. The deadline for proposals for research grants is, so to speak, December 31.

A REMINDER ABOUT SOME
OTHER SOURCES OF WORDINESS

In addition to the sources of wordiness we have examined in this chapter, we should bear in mind that in earlier chapters we touched on some other common sources.

Many of the kinds of metadiscourse, for example, can lead to wordy sentences such as this: *I would like to conclude by noting that, at least in my rather limited way of looking at things, it is important to remember that their deadlines are firm.* Here everything before *their deadlines* is metadiscourse.

The *there is/are* and *it is* constructions can also lead to sentences that are wordier than necessary: *There are many students who never graduate* as opposed to *Many students never graduate.*

Finally, passive verbs also lead to wordier sentences than the corresponding active forms (*The books were stolen by them* as opposed to *They stole the books*). But as we have already seen, sometimes metadiscourse, a *there is/are* or *it is* construction, and a passive verb are necessary. We must all cultivate the ability to distinguish the justified from the unjustified uses of these.

TO REVIEW:
WORDINESS

This chapter shows that many kinds of wordiness are alike in their relationship to given information. Writers sometimes produce wordiness by repeating given information without good reason, including some information that is clearly implied by other information, and using more words than they need to convey certain bits of information. Beyond this, sometimes they use words that in context carry no information at all. You should work to correct the results of such practices as you edit your prose.

IN CONCLUSION

Many people say that their written products are never "finished," that sooner or later they must simply abandon them. Whether this is always true I cannot say. I can say, however, that if you remember the guidelines explained in this book and read and revise your prose with them in mind, your prose will become clearer and more coherent. And when that happens, your prose will be much more nearly "finished."

FURTHER READING

Strunk, William, Jr., and E. B. White (1959), *The Elements of Style* (revised ed.). New York: The Macmillan Company.

Williams, J. M. (1985), "The Grammar of Concision," *Style: Ten Lessons in Clarity and Grace* (2nd ed.). Glenview, IL: Scott, Foresman.

Zinsser, William (1985), *On Writing Well* (3rd ed.). New York: Harper and Row.

Revision Checklist Based on the Guidelines for Clear and Coherent Prose

1. In general, have you kept the topics of consecutive sentences identical or closely related to each other or to material in preceding comments?
2. In general, have you expressed your topics early in sentences or in the grammatical subject?
3. In general, have you expressed the important information in your sentences in their comments and the most important information of all at the end of the comments?
4. In general, have you made it relatively easy for readers to identify your topics and comments in longer and more complicated sentences?
5. In general, have you established coherent sets of topics in major parts of your essay or in your entire essay?
6. In general, have you used a set of topics that is appropriate to the overall method of development you have selected and justified for your essay?
7. In general, have you expressed some given information in your sentences?
8. In general, have you made sure that your given information is easily identifiable by readers?
9. In general, have you marked your bits of given information with the appropriate amount of force?
10. In general, have you expressed given information in your sentences before new information?
11. In general, have you avoided writing sentences that convey only given information or that include words that carry no information?

Glossary of Grammatical Terms

What follows are definitions of the grammatical terms that I use in this book. In the interests of simplicity and conventional usage, I have based these definitions on those from traditional grammar. And they are very brief; I have tried to provide just enough information to refresh your memory about terms that you may have forgotten.

Absolute Phrase

A phrase made up of a noun or a pronoun followed usually by a participle and possibly by some modifiers. It is not connected to the rest of the sentence by a single word, nor does it modify a single word in the rest of the sentence. Rather, it stands in an absolute or independent relationship to the rest of the sentence and modifies all of it. *The storm approaching rapidly, the golfers headed for shelter* begins with the absolute phrase *The storm approaching rapidly.*

Adjective

A word that modifies a noun, pronoun, or a group of words used as a noun. Typically, adjectives modify by describing (a *humid* day), limiting (*two* points), pointing out (*this* tree), or questioning (*which* student?).

Adjective Clause

A group of words that has a subject and a predicate but that cannot stand alone as an independent sentence. Rather, it modifies a noun or a pronoun. In the following sentence, the adjective clause is boldfaced: *The batter **who has the smoothest swing** will win the batting title.* The adjective clause modifies the noun *batter.*

Adverbial Clause

A group of words that has a subject and a predicate but that cannot stand alone as an independent sentence. Rather, it modifies a verb, an adjective, an adverb, or a whole sentence. It modifies by specifying causes, conditions, comparisons, manners, places, purposes, times, and results. In the following sentence, the adverbial clause is boldfaced: ***When you have their attention,*** *you should raise the flag.* It provides an indication of the condition and the time for the raising of the flag.

Agent

Most simply, the person or thing referred to in a sentence that performs the action mentioned in the sentence. More technically, it is the entity that performs an action. In *Jason hit the softball,* the agent is Jason. In *The dam was washed out by the swollen river,* the agent is the river.

Appositive

A word (usually a noun), phrase, or clause used after a noun, noun phrase, or pronoun. Typically the appositive will rename or further describe the person or thing referred to by the noun, noun phrase, or pronoun. A noun used as an appositive is boldfaced in the following sentence: *My old friend **John** has set records in some of the field events in track.* A noun phrase used as an appositive is boldfaced in the following sentence: *Miss Liu, **a most influential teacher,** stressed the importance of phonics.* And a clause used as an appositive is boldfaced in the following sentence: *The fact **that you spoke without thinking** does not totally excuse you.*

Article

A, an, or *the.* These are often also classified as kinds of adjectives.

Clause

A group of words containing a subject and a predicate. If the group expresses a complete thought and can stand alone as a sentence, it is called an independent clause (*Nancy spotted a great blue heron.*). If the group does not express a complete thought and cannot stand alone as a sentence, it is called a dependent or subordinate clause (*Since Nancy spotted a great blue heron . . .*).

Complement

A word or a group of words that completes the meaning of a subject, verb, or object. The most common complements are direct objects, indirect objects, predicate nouns, predicate adjectives, and objective complements.

Complete Predicate

The verb, verb auxiliaries, objects, complements, and attached modifiers in a sentence. In the following sentence, the complete predicate is boldfaced: *Barb **applied for a new job in Boulder.***

Compound Sentence

A sentence made up of at least two independent clauses, usually joined by a coordinating conjunction (*We visited the Straits area, but we did not go to Mackinac Island.*) or by a semicolon (*The dissidents at the rally had much to say; little of it made sense.*).

Conjunction

A word used to connect words or groups of words. The most common conjunctions are coordinating conjunctions and subordinating conjunctions. Coordinating conjunctions (*and, but, or, for, nor, so,* and *yet*) connect elements of equal grammatical stature. Subordinating conjunctions (such as *since* and *although*) connect dependent elements to the independent clause in a sentence.

Connective

A general name for words and phrases that connect words, phrases, clauses, and sentences. The most common connectives are the conjunctions.

Dangling Modifier

A modifier whose implied subject is different from the subject of the following clause. The introductory phrase in *Dripping from the mouth of the fish, my sons were repulsed by the blood* dangles since its implied subject (*the blood*) is different from the subject of the following clause (*my sons*).

Dependent Clause

A group of words that contains a subject and a predicate but that does not express a complete thought and that cannot stand by itself as a sentence. Dependent or subordinate clauses function as nouns, adjectives, or adverbs within sentences. The boldfaced dependent clause in the following sentence functions as a noun in being the subject: **What you propose** *is impossible.*

Direct Object

A noun, pronoun, or other group of words acting as a noun that receives the action described in the verb or is directly affected by the action named in the verb. For example, in *Steve caught the trout*, the direct object is *the trout*.

Expletive

A word, such as *it* or *there*, that is followed by a form of *to be* and that introduces a subject or an object: **There** *are agates along the shoreline east of Grand Marais. There* introduces *agates.*

Gerund

A kind of verbal that functions as a noun. In the following sentence, the gerund *studying* functions as the subject: **Studying** *never interferes with their education.*

Independent Clause

A group of words that has a subject and a predicate, that expresses a complete thought, and that can stand independently as a sentence. For example: *Denise works as an aide in the elementary school.*

Indirect Object

A word or words showing to whom something is given or to or for whom something is done. *Us* is the indirect object in the following sentence: *Mary Ann gave* **us** *her address in London.*

Infinitive

The base form of a verb (for example, *talk*) preceded by *to*, the infinitive marker. Infinitives can be used as nouns, adjectives, or adverbs. In the following sentence, *to buy* is used as an adjective modifying *the book*: *The book **to buy** is "The Name of the Columbine."*

Infinitive Phrase

An infinitive and its subject, complements, or modifiers. Infinitive phrases function as nouns, adjectives, and adverbs. In the following sentence, *to be in town before the rush hour* is used as an adverb modifying the verb *left*: *Diane left early **to be in town before the rush hour.***

Linking Verb

Linking verbs make a statement by indicating a state of being or a condition. Linking verbs are used to link the subject with a noun or pronoun (the predicate noun) that renames it (*Michelle **is** the assistant*), or to link the subject with an adjective (the predicate adjective) that describes it (*Michelle **is** efficient.*).

Modifier

A word or group of words that limits or qualifies the meaning of another word or group of words. The most common modifiers are adjectives (a *beautiful* sunset) and adverbs (ran *vigorously*).

Nominalization

A noun that is derived from or that carries essentially the same content as a verb or an adjective. For example, from the verb *analyze* we can derive the noun *analysis*, and from the adjective *cheerful* we derive the noun *cheerfulness*.

Noun

A word that names a person (*Christopher*), place (*Traverse City*), thing (*boat*), quality (*kindness*), or idea (*freedom*).

Noun Clause

A group of words that has a subject and a predicate but that cannot stand alone as an independent sentence. Rather, it functions within a sentence as nouns do. For example, in the following sentence the noun clause is boldfaced: ***What they did** is splendid.* This noun clause serves as the subject of the sentence.

Noun Phrase

A group of words usually consisting of an article (*a*, *an*, *the*), one or more modifiers, and a noun (*the crumbling roadway*). Noun phrases function within sentences as nouns do. In the following sentence, one noun phrase serves as the subject, and another serves as the direct object: **The militant child** *refused* **the new pacifier.**

Object

A noun, pronoun, or a group of words acting as a noun that receives the action of or is affected by a verb, verbal, or a preposition. The most common objects are direct objects (*He found* **his bat**.), indirect objects (*She gave* **Tom** *a volume of poetry*.), and objects of prepositions (*They drove to* **the coast**.).

Objective Complement

A noun or an adjective that completes the action of certain verbs and refers to or describes the direct object. For example, *chairman* is the objective complement in *They elected Paul chairman*, as is *rude* in *They considered him rude.*

Participial Phrase

A participle and its object, as well as any modifiers. Participial phrases function as adjectives. For example, in the following sentence the boldfaced participial phrase modifies *the fiddler*: **Playing a forlorn tune**, *the fiddler walked into the shadows.*

Participle

A kind of verbal that functions as an adjective. There are present participles (the *singing* dog) and past participles (the *neglected* book, the *broken* bike). In addition, participles can be active (*studying*) or passive (*being studied*).

Passive Voice

Transitive verbs are in the passive voice when their subjects receive the action named by them. For example: *A new syllabus was provided by the committee.*

Periodic Sentence

A sentence in which the main thought or the subject and the verb of the independent clause do not appear until near the end. The following is a relatively short periodic sentence: *Noses testing the wind, ears tensed for any signs of danger, the deer walked from the cedar trees into the field of alfalfa.*

Phrase

A group of words that lacks a subject and a predicate and that cannot make a statement. The most common phrases are noun phrases, verb phrases, adjective phrases, adverb phrases, and prepositional phrases.

Predicate Adjective

An adjective that follows a linking verb and describes the subject (*Jerry is* **astute***.*).

Predicate Noun

A noun that follows a linking verb and renames or refers back to the subject (*Roger is the* **boss***.*).

Prepositional Phrase

A preposition followed by a noun or a pronoun that serves as its object, together with its modifiers. The prepositional phrase in the following sentence is boldfaced: *He steered the boat* **toward the new dock***.*

Subject

A noun or a word group acting as a noun with which the verb in a sentence agrees in person and in number. In the following sentence, *I* is the subject: **I** *believe in them.*

Verb

A word that usually expresses an action (*ran*) or a state of being (*is*). Verbs may be transitive or intransitive. With transitive verbs the action is directed toward a receiver (*He drove the truck.*). With intransitive verbs the action is not directed toward a receiver (*She was singing.*).

Verbal

A word that is constructed from a verb but that functions as another part of speech. The verbals include gerunds, participles, and infinitives.

Index